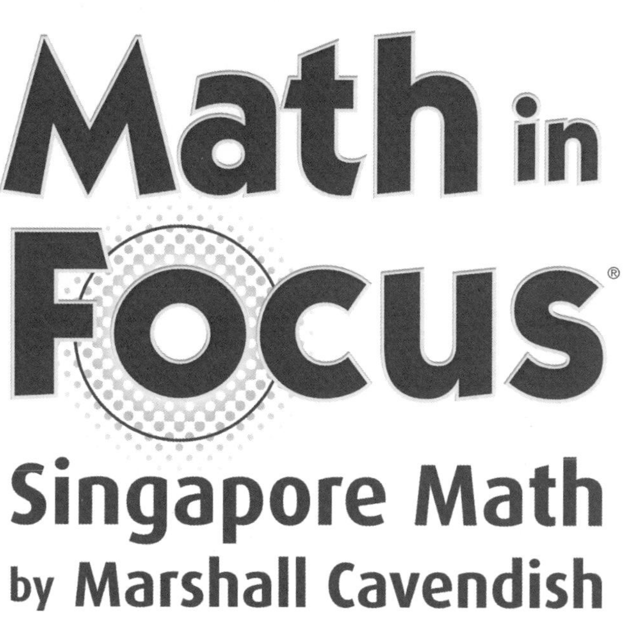

Enrichment

Consultant and Author
Dr. Fong Ho Kheong

Author
Ang Kok Cheng

US Distributor

Published by Marshall Cavendish Education
An imprint of Marshall Cavendish International (Singapore) Private Limited
Times Centre, 1 New Industrial Road, Singapore 536196
Customer Service Hotline: (65) 6411 0820
E-mail: tmesales@sg.marshallcavendish.com
Website: www.marshallcavendish.com/education

Distributed by
Houghton Mifflin Harcourt
222 Berkeley Street
Boston, MA 02116
Tel: 617-351-5000
Website: www.hmheducation.com/mathinfocus

First published 2009
2013 Edition

Math in Focus® Enrichment 4B
ISBN 978-0-669-01583-6

Printed in Singapore

1 2 3 4 5 6 7 8 1897 18 17 16 15 14 13
4500354349 A B C D E

Contents

Introducing

Math in Focus®

Enrichment

Written to complement *Math in Focus®: Singapore Math by Marshall Cavendish* Grade 4, exercises in *Enrichment 4A* and *4B* are designed for advanced students seeking a challenge beyond the exercises and questions in the Student Books and Workbooks.

These exercises require children to draw on their fundamental mathematical understanding as well as recently acquired concepts and skills, combining problem-solving strategies with critical thinking skills.

Critical thinking skills enhanced by working on *Enrichment* exercises include classifying, comparing, sequencing, analyzing parts and whole, identifying patterns and relationships, induction (from specific to general), deduction (from general to specific), and spatial visualization.

One set of problems is provided for each chapter, to be assigned after the chapter has been completed. *Enrichment* exercises can be assigned while other students are working on the Chapter Review/Test, or while the class is working on subsequent chapters.

BLANK

Name: ______________________ Date: ______________

Decimals

Thinking Skills

Write the length of $\overline{AB}$ in decimal form.

1. A ——————————————————— B

0 cm 1 2 3 4 5 6 7 8 9 10 11 12

$AB =$ __________ cm

Study the number line and answer the questions.

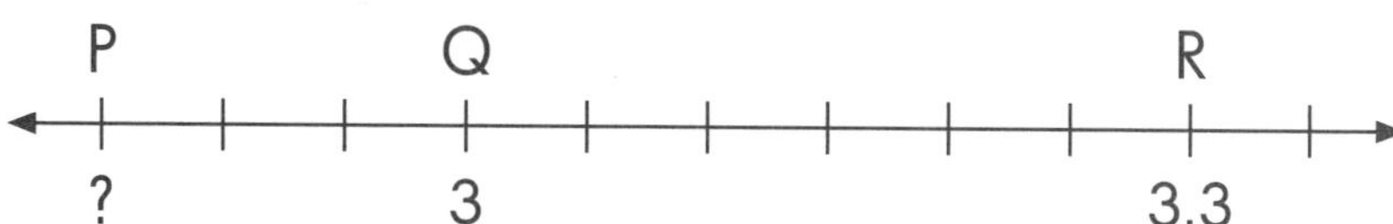

2. What number does point P represent?

____

3. Round P to the nearest tenth.

____

Name: ______________________ Date: ______________

Compare and order the numbers.

4. Write the numbers in order from least to greatest.

6.9 $6\frac{1}{2}$ $6\frac{1}{4}$ 6.1

____

5. Write the numbers in order from greatest to least.

7.2 $7\frac{2}{5}$ $6\frac{3}{5}$ 6.5

____

Solve.

6. Johnson's height is 1.1 meters when rounded to the nearest tenth of a meter. What could his height be?

Name: ______________________ Date: ______________

Fill in the blanks. Then write the missing letters in the table. An example is shown.

7. ___0.9___ more than 6.02 is 6.92. (C)

a. 0.05 more than ________ is 4.73. (E)

b. 0.6 less than 2.98 is ________. (M)

c. 0.06 less than ________ is 8.27. (L)

d. ________ more than 7.5 is 8.2. (I)

e. 0.09 more than 1.93 is ________. (D)

f. 0.08 less than ________ is 9.04. (A)

g.

Letter			C				
Number	2.02	4.68	0.9	0.7	2.38	9.12	8.33

Name: ______________________ Date: ______________

Complete the pattern.

8. $4\frac{1}{2}$ 5.55 $6\frac{3}{5}$ ________ ________ 9.75

Solve. Show your work.

9. Louis had a sum of money. He spent $0.75 on a notebook, 25 cents on an eraser, and $0.80 on a ruler. He had 20 cents left. How much money did Louis have at first?

10. Paul is 0.86 meter tall. George is 0.2 meter taller than Paul but 0.05 meter shorter than Leon. How tall is Leon?

Name: ______________________ Date: ______________

Exploration

Write each decimal in three ways.

11. 3.27 = 3 ones and 27 hundredths

= ______________________

= ______________________

= ______________________

12. 4.587 = 4 ones and 5 tenths 8 hundredths 7 thousandths

= ______________________

= ______________________

= ______________________

Solve.

13. Five decimals form a pattern when arranged in order.
Three of these decimals are shown below.
Find all possible pairs of decimals to form a pattern.

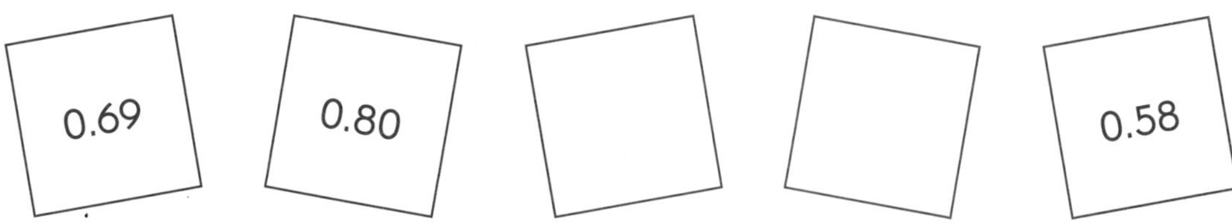

Name: ________________________ Date: ________________

The statements below are incorrect. Write the correct statements.

14. In 14.238, the value of the digit 1 is ten, and the value of the digit 3 is tenth.

____

15. 2.409 is the same as 2 ones and 4 tenths 9 hundredths.

____

16. 9.3 more than 0.2 is the same as 9.3 > 0.2.

____

Find the rule for each number pattern. Then complete the pattern.

17. 0.42 0.53 0.64 ________ ________

Rule: ____

18. 7.95 7.71 7.47 ________ ________

Rule: ____

19. 0.06 0.12 0.24 ________ ________

Rule: ____

Name: ______________________ Date: ______________

Adding and Subtracting Decimals

Solve.

1. Each letter stands for a different digit. Find the digit that each letter stands for. Use the digits 1, 2, 3, and 5.

$$A.CB + B.BC = C.DD$$

2. The sum of the numbers on each side of the triangle is 13.2. Fill in the circles with the given decimals.

1.2 2.4 3.6 4.8 6 7.2

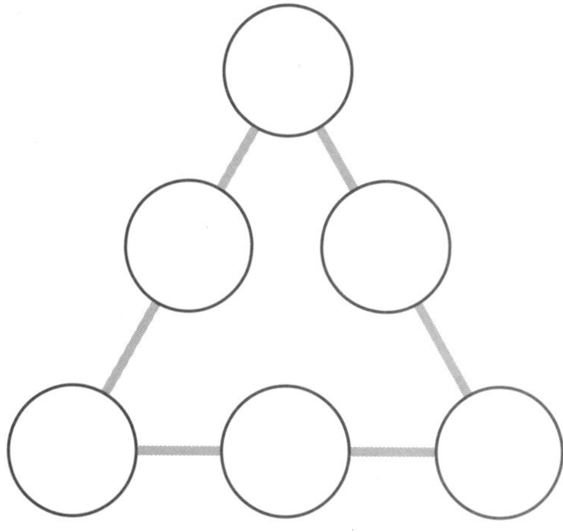

Name: ______________________ Date: ______________

Solve. Show your work.

3. The table shows the fees for the hotel parking garage. Mr. Spencer parked his car from 1:00 P.M. to 5:14 P.M. How much did Mr. Spencer have to pay to park his car?

Schedule	Charges
1:00 P.M. to 5:00 P.M.	\$2.50 an hour or part of an hour
After 5:00 P.M.	\$4.00 an hour or part of an hour

4. Lee spent \$4.30 on a plate of spaghetti, \$1.25 on a bottle of fruit juice, and \$3.45 on a fountain pen. Lee had \$50 at first. How much money did she have left?

Name: ______________________ Date: ______________

Solve. Show your work.

Mrs. Kemery bought some canned food from a shop. She bought one can of each type of food. The table shows the prices of the canned food.

Canned Food	Price (one can)
Fruit Cocktail	\$3.50
Condensed Milk	95¢
Tuna	\$2.32
Pineapple	\$11.27

5. How much cheaper is a can of tuna than a can of fruit cocktail?

6. Mrs. Kemery bought an extra can of pineapple and a can of fruit cocktail. How much did Mrs. Kemery spend altogether?

Name: ______________________ Date: ______________

Strategies

Solve. Show your work.

7. Morgan saved \$3.85 on Friday.
He saved \$2.20 more on Saturday than on Friday.
The amount Morgan saved on Sunday was equal to the total amount of money he saved on both Friday and Saturday.
How much did Morgan save altogether on Saturday and Sunday?

8. Mrs. Blaine had 0.95 pound of chicken in the fridge, but she decided to buy some more. She used 2.75 pounds of chicken to make some stew and minced 1.42 pounds of chicken for a Shepherd's pie. She was left with 1.35 pounds of chicken. How much chicken did Mrs. Blaine buy?

Name: ______________________ **Date:** ______________

9. Natalie is 1.32 meters tall.
Her younger brother Eric is 0.38 meter shorter than she is.
Their father is 0.45 meter taller than Natalie.
What is the total height of the three of them?

Name: ______________________ Date: ______________

Exploration

Solve.

10. Find all possible values of A, B, and C. Each letter stands for a different digit.

$$\begin{array}{r} 0.\ C\ A \\ +\ 0.\ 2\ B \\ \hline 1.\ 0\ 1 \end{array}$$

11. Find all possible values of X, Y, and Z. Each letter stands for a different digit.

$$\begin{array}{r} 1.\ X\ Y \\ -\ 0.\ Z\ 9 \\ \hline 0.\ 6\ 1 \end{array}$$

Name: ______________________ **Date:** ______________

Journal Writing

Number the steps in the correct order.

12. Write 1, 2, 3, and 4 in the boxes to show the steps for adding the two decimals.

$$
\begin{array}{r}
0.56 \\
+\ 0.73 \\
\hline
1.29
\end{array}
$$

☐ Add the ones.

☐ Regroup the tenths.

☐ Add the tenths.

☐ Add the hundredths.
No regrouping is required.

Name: ______________________ Date: ______________

Write the steps.

13. Write the steps needed to add the six decimals.

0.83 + 0.17 + 0.45 + 0.55 + 0.96 + 0.04

Step 1 ______________________

____

____

Step 2 ______________________

____

____

Step 3 ______________________

____

____

Step 4 ______________________

____

____

Name: ______________________ Date: ______________

Write the steps.

14. Write the steps needed to subtract the decimals.

$$\begin{array}{r} 1.47 \\ -\ 0.98 \\ \hline 0.49 \end{array}$$

Step 1 ______________________________

____

____

Step 2 ______________________________

____

____

Step 3 ______________________________

____

____

Step 4 ______________________________

____

____

Name: ______________________ Date: ______________

Angles

Thinking Skills

Solve.

1. How many more angles measuring less than 90° are there in Figure A than in Figure B?

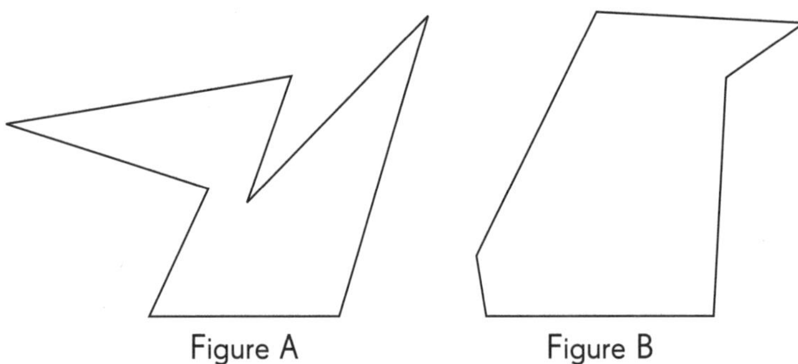

Figure A Figure B

2. Measure and list the angles in order from the smallest angle to the largest angle.

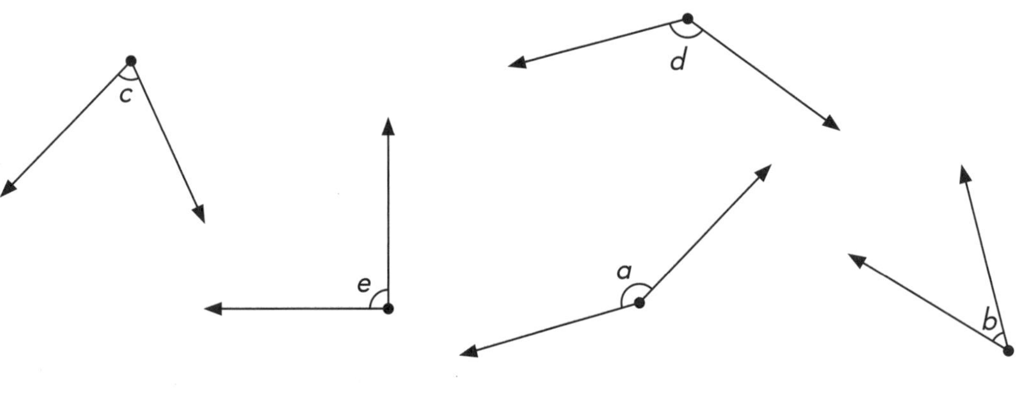

______ ______ ______ ______ ______

Smallest Largest

Name: ______________________ Date: ______________

Solve. Show your work.

3. Mary started her piano lesson at 5:20 P.M. The lesson ended at 7:05 P.M. How many $\frac{1}{4}$-turns did the minute hand of the clock move through during this time?

Name: ______________________ Date: ______________

Solve. Show your work.

4. Use a protractor to draw an angle that is one right angle greater than $\angle w$. Label the angle as $\angle AOC$. What is the measure of this new angle?

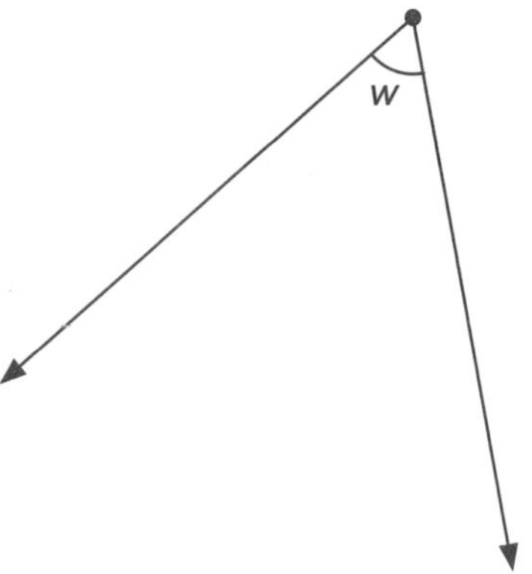

5. $\overleftrightarrow{AB}$ is a line. Draw an angle, $\angle COD$, that has a measure of 125°. The measure of $\angle AOC$ is 30°. What is the measure of $\angle DOB$?

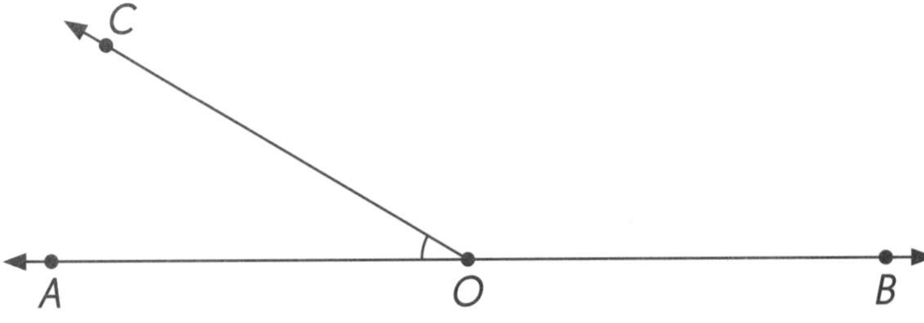

Name: ______________________ Date: ______________

Solve.

6. The measure of angle A is twice as great as the measure of angle B, and the measure of angle C is 3 times the measure of angle B. The measure of angle D is half of the measure of angle C, and the measure of angle A is 36° greater than the measure of angle B. Find the measure of angle D.

Draw.

7. After turning $\frac{3}{4}$-turn clockwise, $1\frac{1}{2}$-turns counterclockwise, and then another $\frac{1}{4}$-turn clockwise, the arrow rests in this final position.

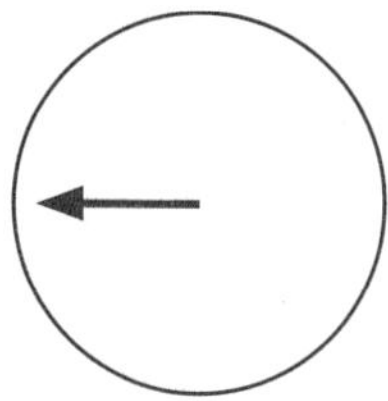

Draw the original position of the arrow.

Name: ______________________ Date: ______________

PROBLEM SOLVING
Exploration

Solve.

8. Arjun is facing north. He wants to end up facing west. Arjun can only use $\frac{1}{2}$-turns, $\frac{1}{4}$-turns, and $\frac{3}{4}$-turns. List three ways that Arjun can turn to end up facing west.

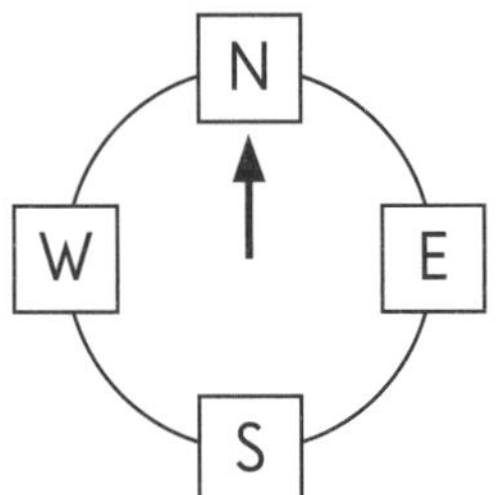

Think of turning once, twice, or three times, and of turning in different directions.

a. ______________________

b. ______________________

c. ______________________

9. Find the unknown angle measure with the help of a protractor.
Describe the method you used to find the angle measure.

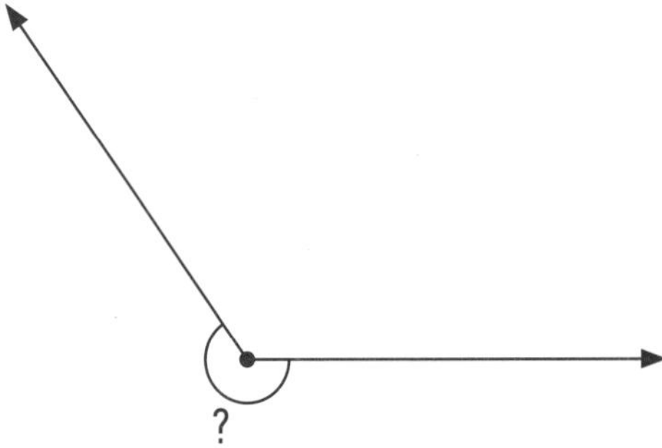

____

____

Name: ______________________ Date: ______________

Number the steps in the correct order. Then draw the angle.

10. Write 1, 2, 3, and 4 in the boxes to show the steps for drawing a 145° angle. Then draw a 145° angle in the space provided.

☐ Place the base line of the protractor on the line and the center of the base line on the point.

☐ Remove the protractor. Draw a ray from the point on the line to the dot.

☐ Use the outer scale to find the 145° mark. Mark it with a dot.

☐ Draw a line and mark a point on the line.

Name: ______________________ Date: ______________

Write a short description.

11. Describe how you can get from point A to point K on the grid below.

Use $\frac{1}{4}$-*turn*, $\frac{1}{2}$-*turn*, and $\frac{3}{4}$-*turn* in your description.

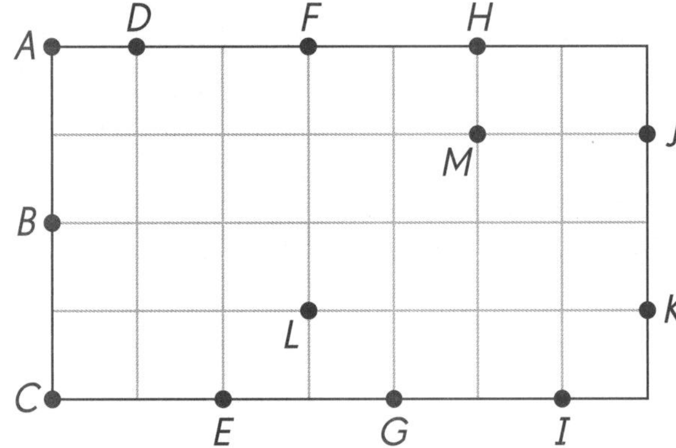

____

____

____

____

____

____

____

Name: ______________________ Date: ______________

Perpendicular and Parallel Line Segments

Thinking Skills

Answer the questions.

1. Which letters have a set of perpendicular line segments?

A H K L U O E F

2. Which letters have a set of parallel line segments?

Y P S I M W Q H

Name: ______________________ Date: ______________

Study the figure carefully and use it to do Exercises 3 to 5.

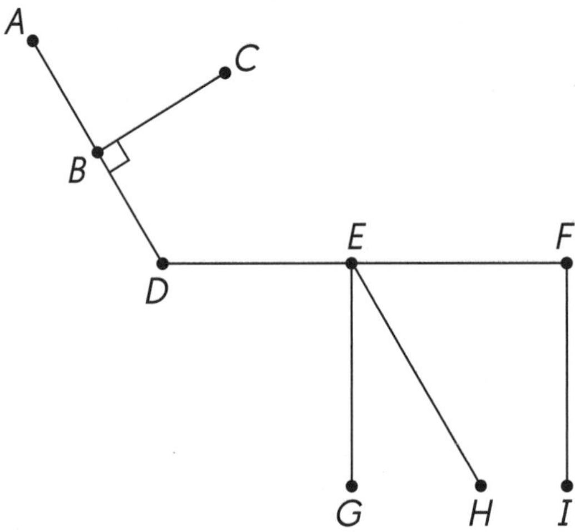

3. $\overline{AD}$ is most likely parallel to __________.

4. Put a cross (✗) beside the statements that are false.

a. $\overline{AB} \parallel \overline{CB}$ __________

b. $\overline{DF} \perp \overline{EG}$ __________

c. $\overline{EH} \perp \overline{AD}$ __________

d. $\overline{EG} \parallel \overline{IF}$ __________

5. What is the total number of pairs of parallel line segments that can be found in the figure?

Name: ______________________ Date: ______________

Draw.

6. Caroline wants to divide the rectangle into 4 identical right triangles and a square using 2 pairs of parallel line segments. Draw the 2 pairs of parallel line segments to show how she can do this.

7. Benjamin has a rectangular picture.
He wants to frame it with a rectangular frame.
In the figure, 2 sides of the frame have been drawn.
Complete the frame by drawing the remaining 2 line segments accurately.

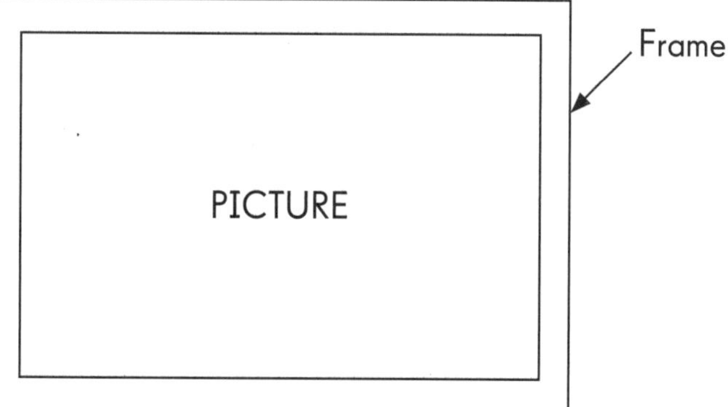

Name: ______________________ Date: ______________

Draw.

8. Use a drawing triangle and a straightedge to draw a line segment parallel to $\overline{AB}$ at point C. Then draw another line segment parallel to $\overline{BC}$ at point A. Extend each line segment until they meet. Label the point of intersection D.

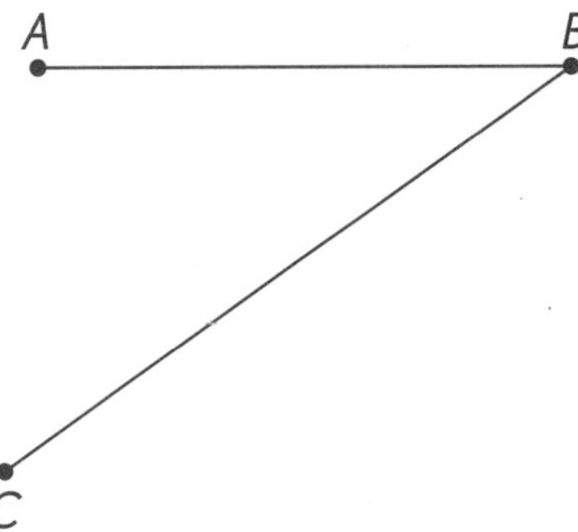

9. The figure is made up of two identical 4-centimeter squares overlapping each other. Draw the figure to scale in the space provided.

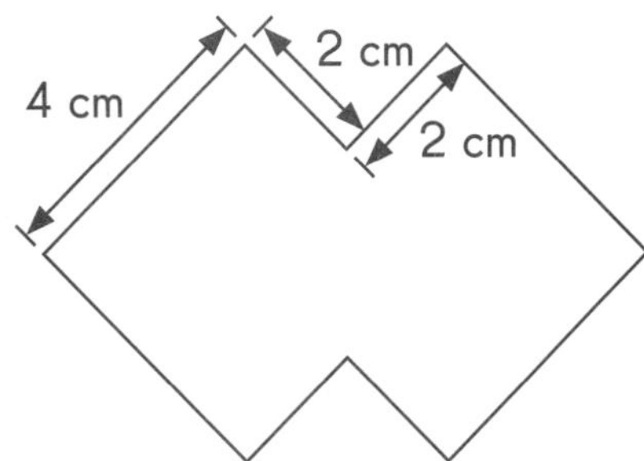

Name: ______________________ Date: ______________

Answer the questions.

10. The figures below are arranged in a pattern.
How many horizontal and vertical line segments will there be in figure D7 altogether?

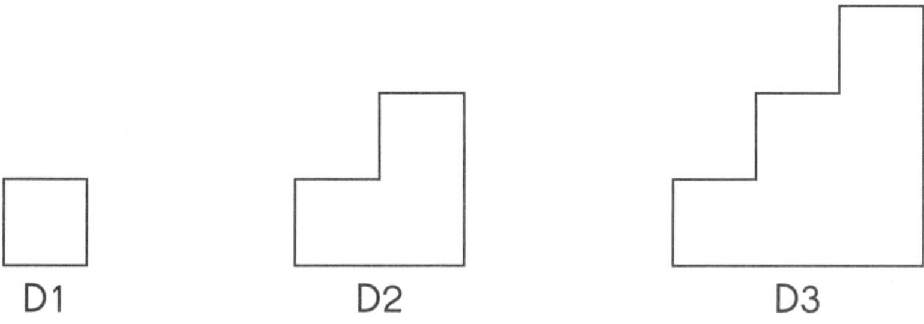

11. Figure A is drawn using 2 horizontal and 5 vertical line segments. Figure B is drawn using 3 horizontal and 2 vertical line segments. There are 9 figures altogether with a total of 21 horizontal and 36 vertical line segments.
How many figure A's are there?

Name: ______________________________ Date: ____________________

Exploration

Draw.

12. Draw as many squares as possible. Use $\overline{AB}$ as one side of each square. How many squares can you draw?

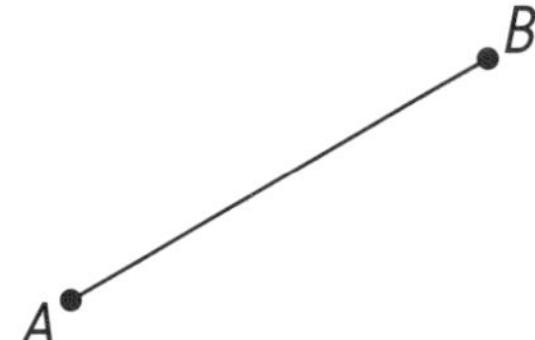

Name: ______________________ Date: ______________

Draw.

13. Draw four rectangles. Use $\overline{AB}$ as one side of each rectangle.

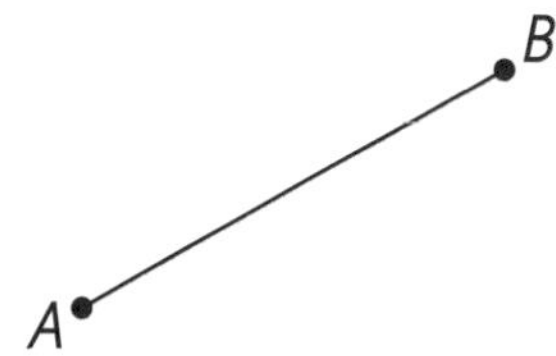

Name: ____________________ **Date:** ________________

Draw.

14. Draw six squares. Use each side of the right triangle as a side for two squares.

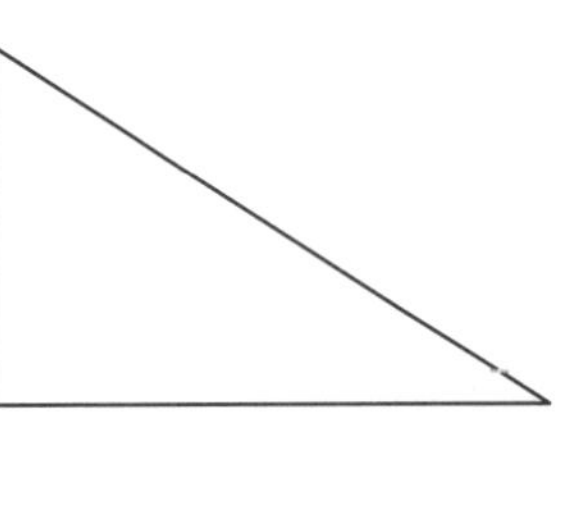

Name: ______________________ Date: ______________

Explain.

15. Explain how you would draw a line segment parallel to $\overline{BC}$ and a line segment perpendicular to $\overline{BC}$.

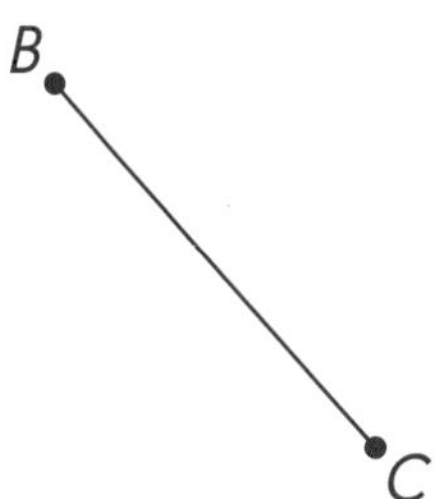

Parallel line segment:

____

____

____

____

____

Perpendicular line segment:

____

____

____

____

____

Name: ______________________ Date: ______________

Describe.

16. Describe this shape using the words *parallel* and *perpendicular.*

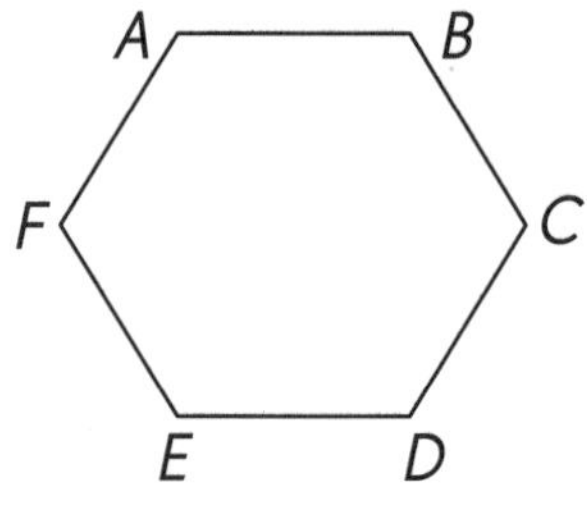

____

____

____

17. Think of a shape with 5 sides or more. Draw the shape and describe it using the words *parallel* and *perpendicular.*

____

____

____

Name: ______________________ **Date:** ______________

Squares and Rectangles

Solve. Show your work.

1. The figure is made up of 9 identical rectangles.
The length of each identical rectangle is twice its width.
Find the perimeter of two of these identical rectangles.

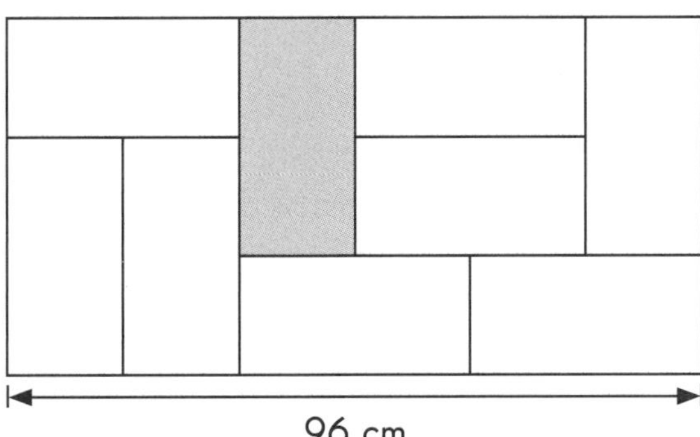

Name: ______________________ Date: ______________

Solve. Show your work.

2. The figure below is made up of rectangle $ABCD$ and square $EFGH$. $EC = CH$. Find the total length of $\overline{BE}$, $\overline{EF}$, and $\overline{CH}$.

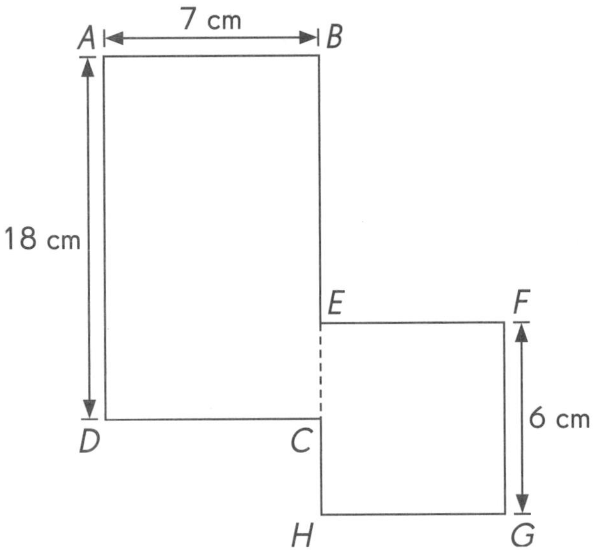

3. A school wants to fence its field. The fence will run along the sides and the back of the tool shed. The length of the tool shed is one third the length of the field, and the width of the tool shed is one quarter the width of the field. How many meters of fencing, excluding a 4-meter gate, must the school order?

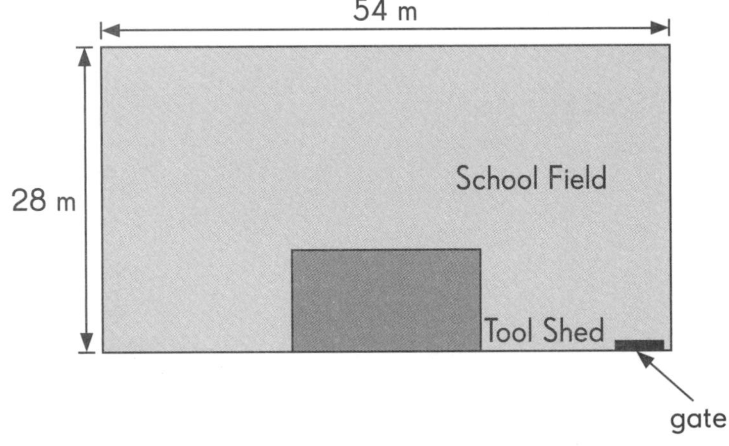

Name: ______________________ **Date:** ______________

Solve. Show your work.

4. The perimeter of rectangle *ABCD* is twice the perimeter of square *EFGH*. What is the length of rectangle *ABCD*?
The figures are not drawn to scale.

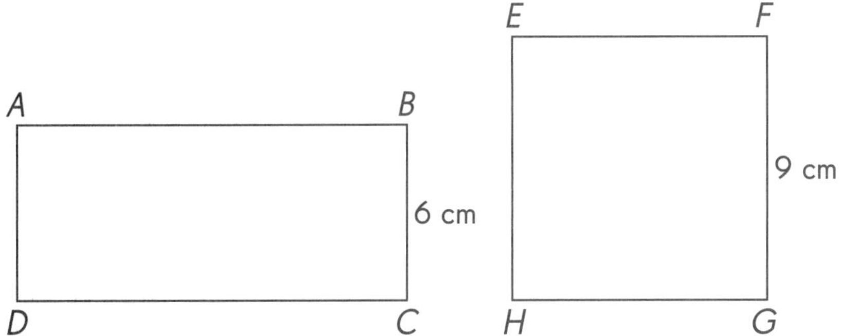

5. The figure is made up of 5 squares. Each side of square A is 6 centimeters long, each side of square B is 4 centimeters long, and each side of square C is 5 centimeters long. Find the total length around the figure.

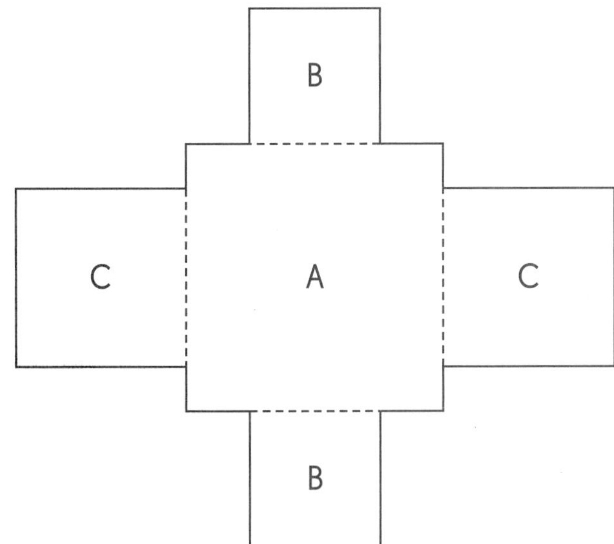

Name: ______________________ Date: ______________

Solve. Show your work.

6. The figure shows three identical squares.
Find the sum of the measures of $\angle a$ and $\angle b$.

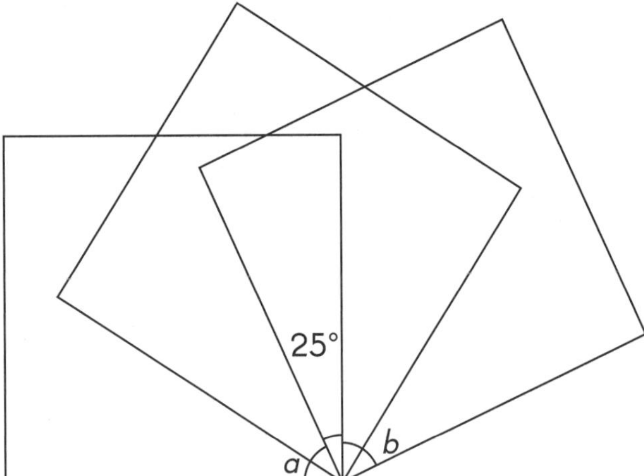

Name: ______________________ **Date:** ______________

Solve. Show your work.

7. Figure *ABCD* is a square. The measure of ∠*a* is twice the measure of ∠*b*. Find the measure of ∠*a*.

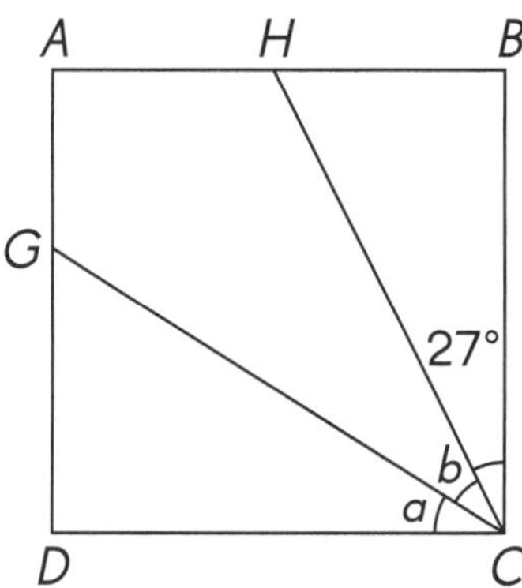

8. The figure, not drawn to scale, is a square. The measure of ∠*c* is half of the measure of ∠*a*. The measure of ∠*b* is 20° less than the measure of ∠*a*. Find the sum of the measures of ∠*a* and ∠*b*.

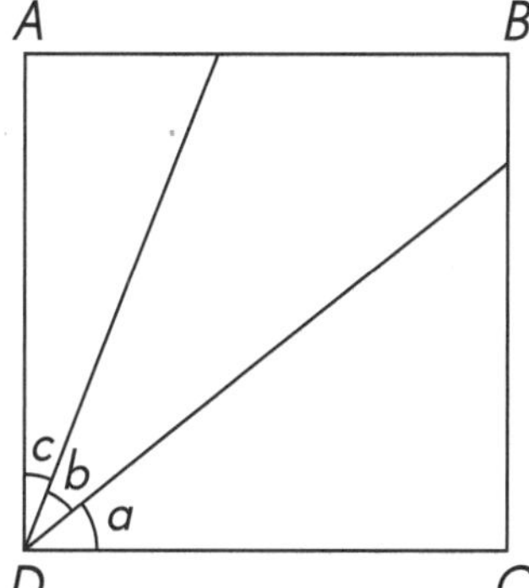

Name: ______________________ Date: ______________

Exploration

Solve.

9. Find the total number of rectangles and the total number of squares in the figure.

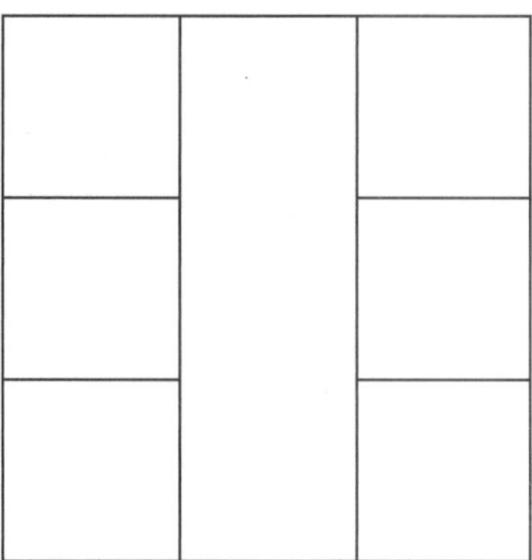

10. Trace and cut out the squares and rectangles below. Use the cut-outs to make 4 different figures.

Name: ______________________ Date: ______________

Answer the question.

11. Draw 2 line segments in each rectangle so that each line segment touches any two sides of the rectangle. Mark all the angles. How many angles are there in each case?

Name: ______________________ Date: ______________

Compare.

12. Write down all the properties of squares and rectangles. Compare them and circle the common properties.

Square	Rectangle
______________	______________
______________	______________
______________	______________
______________	______________
______________	______________
______________	______________
______________	______________
______________	______________
______________	______________
______________	______________

Name: ______________________ Date: ______________

List the steps.

13. The figure is made up of line segments that meet at right angles. Write the steps you used to find the lengths of $\overline{GH}$ and $\overline{DE}$.

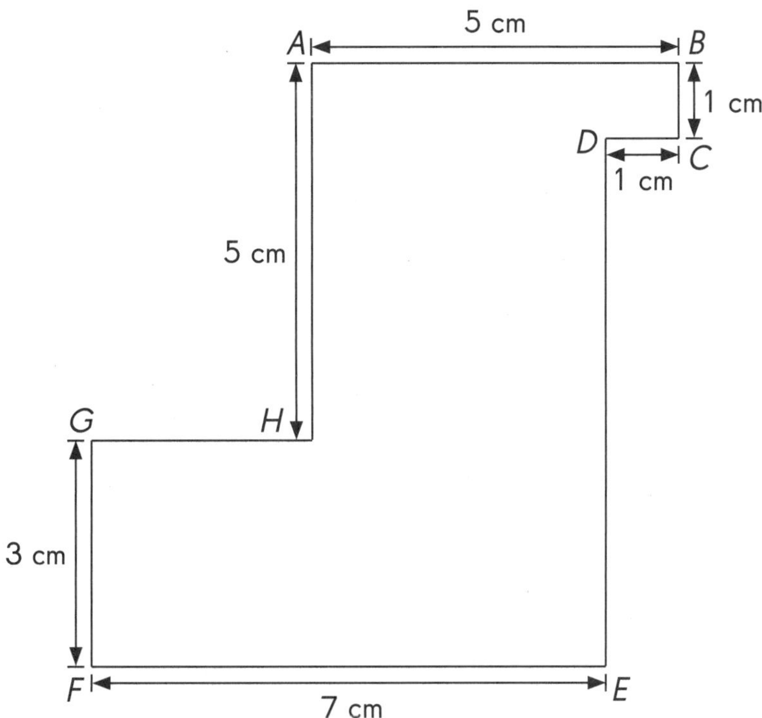

Name: ______________________ Date: ______________

Area and Perimeter

Thinking Skills

Solve. Show your work.

1. Each edge of a cube is 9 centimeters long.
Find the total length of all the edges of the cube.

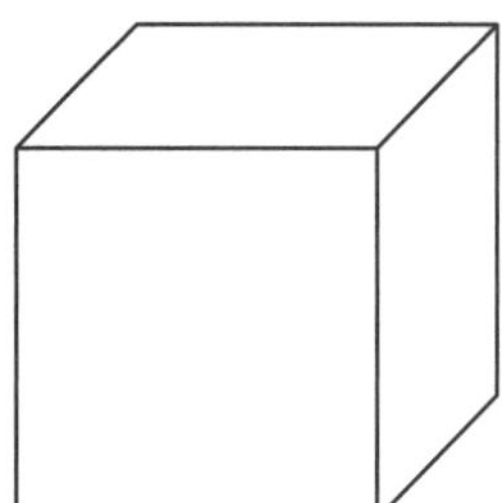

2. A rectangle has a perimeter of 140 centimeters. Its length is 4 times its width. Find the area of the rectangle.

Name: ______________________ Date: ______________

Solve. Show your work.

3. Jack needs to run a distance of 800 meters around a rectangular field. The field is 65 meters long and 15 meters wide. How many times must Jack run around the field?

4. The figure below is not drawn to scale. *ABCD* and *EFGC* are rectangles, and *GHIC* is a square. *BE* = *EC*. Find the perimeter of the whole figure.

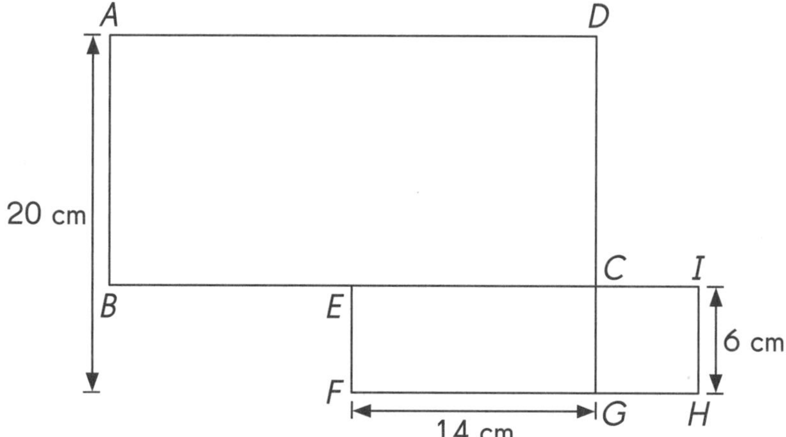

Name: ______________________ Date: ______________

Solve. Show your work.

5. A rectangular piece of paper measures 13 centimeters by 9 centimeters. Estimate the number of squares, each with a side length of 4 centimeters, that can be cut from the piece of paper.

6. The figure below is made up of 6 identical rectangles. Each of these identical rectangles has a width that is half its length. The area of the figure is 768 square centimeters. Find the perimeter of one of the six rectangles.

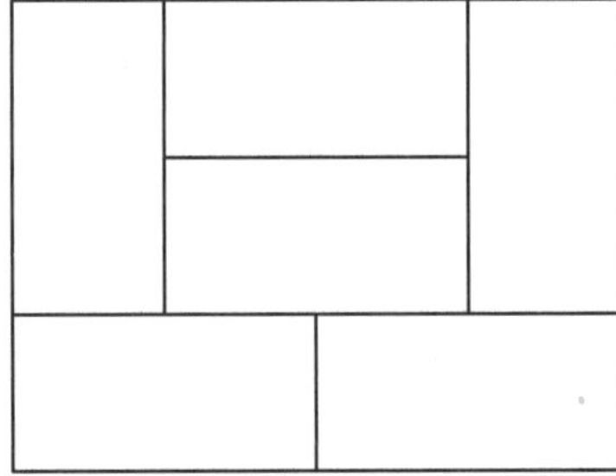

Name: ______________________ Date: ______________

Solve. Show your work.

7. The length of a rectangle was 6 times its width. When the length was increased by 6 centimeters, the area became 36 square centimeters. Then, when the width was increased by 4 centimeters, the new width became 6 centimeters. What was the perimeter of the rectangle at first?

8. The area of rectangle B is half of the area of rectangle A.
The width of A is two-thirds its length.
The width of B is three-quarters its length.
The width of A is the same as the length of B, and the area of A is between 60 square centimeters and 100 square centimeters.
Find the lengths of both rectangles.

Name: ______________________ Date: ______________

Solve. Show your work.

9. The figure is made up of squares of different sizes.
The side length of each square is half the side length of the next square.
The area of square A is 9 square centimeters.
What is the perimeter of the largest square?

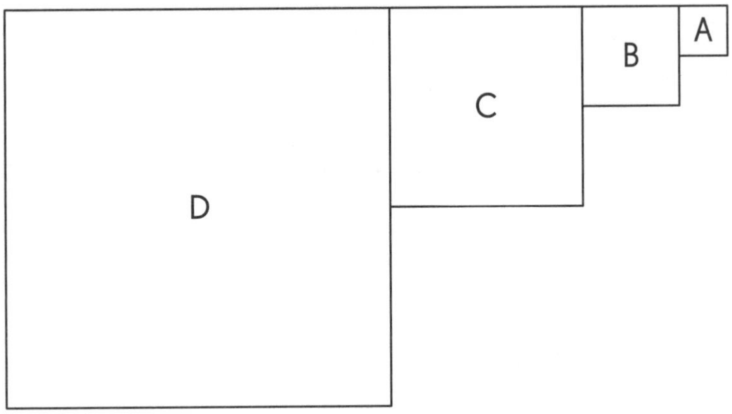

D C B A

Name: ______________________ Date: ______________

Exploration

Answer the questions.

Use a geoboard and a rubber band. Make as many figures as you can that have an area of 12 square centimeters. Find the length, width, and perimeter of each figure. Record the lengths, widths, and perimeters in the table.
If you do not have a geoboard, you can use grids. Shade the different figures on separate grids.

Figure	1	2	3	4	5	6
Area	12	12	12	12	12	12
Length						
Width						
Perimeter						

10. What is the minimum perimeter of the figures you have made?
Can you make another figure with a smaller perimeter?

11. What is the maximum perimeter of the figures you have made?
Can you make another figure with a larger perimeter?

12. Describe any pattern you observe.

Name: ______________________ Date: ______________

13. In each figure, draw line segments to divide the figure into squares or rectangles. Each line segment should touch at least one corner of the figure. Number the shapes you have identified.

a.

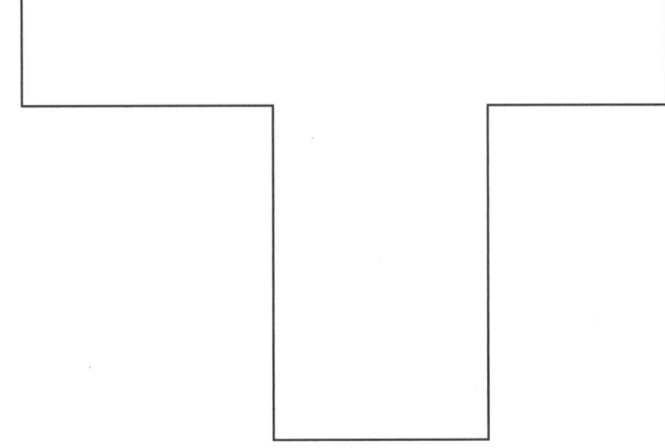

b.

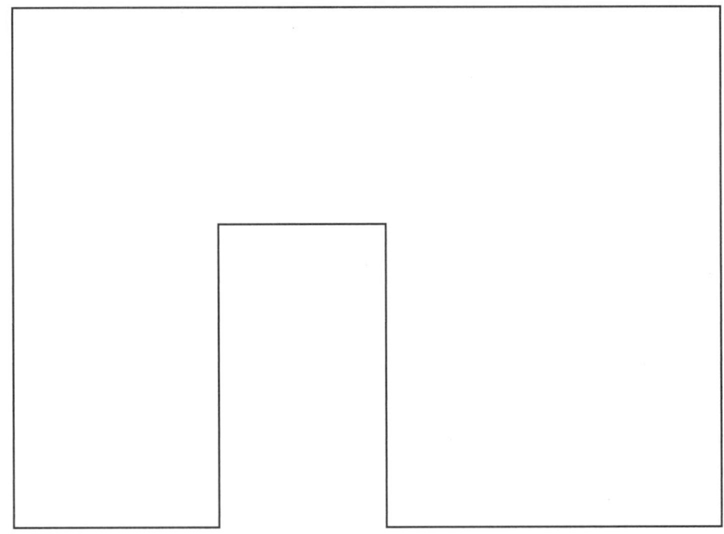

Name: ______________________ Date: ______________

Write the steps.

14. Find the perimeter of the figure. Write the steps you use to find the perimeter.

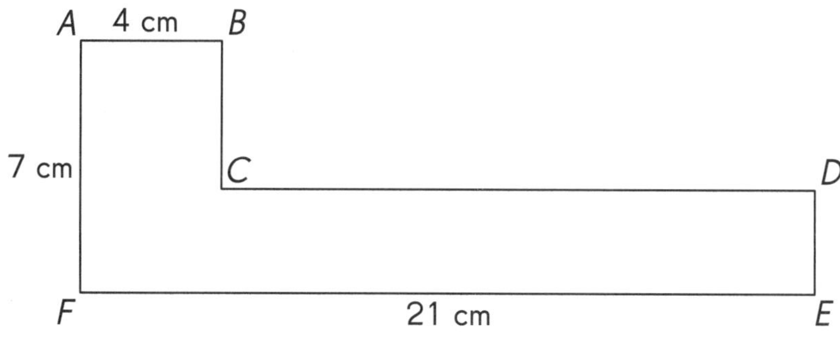

15. The outer rectangle is 48 centimeters long and 24 centimeters wide.
The path around the inner rectangle is 3 centimeters wide.
Find the area of the inner rectangle.
Write the steps you use to find the area.

Name: ______________________ Date: ______________

Symmetry

Thinking Skills

Solve.

1. Draw a line of symmetry on the figure.

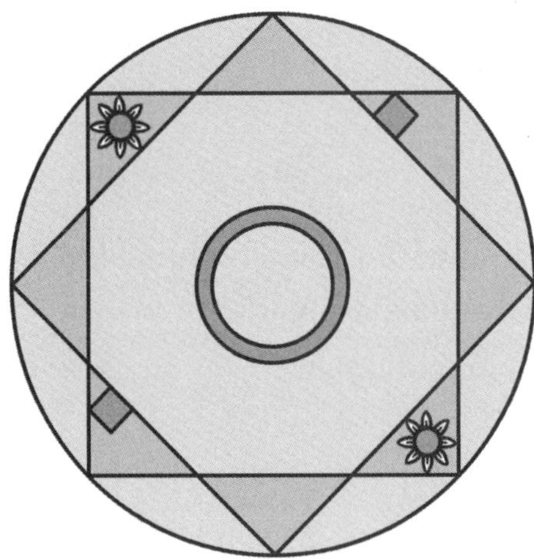

2. All sides of the figure are equal in length. How many lines of symmetry are there in the figure?

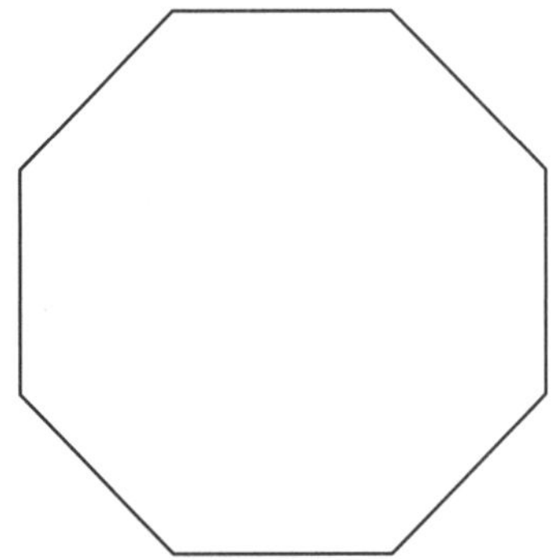

Name: ______________________ Date: ______________

Shade.

3. The figure is made up of 25 squares. Shade 5 more squares so that the figure has 4 lines of symmetry.

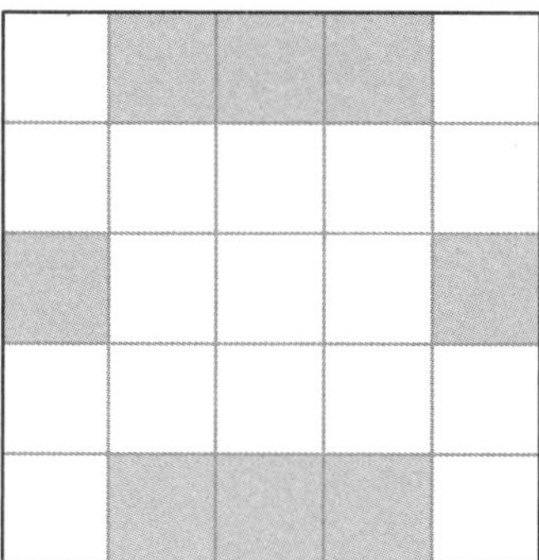

4. Shade the figures that have rotational symmetry and at least one line of symmetry.

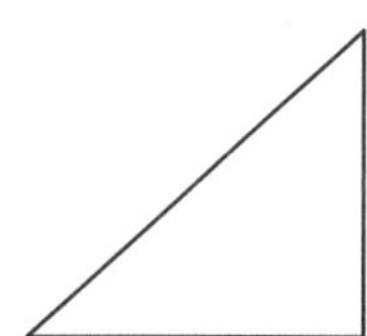
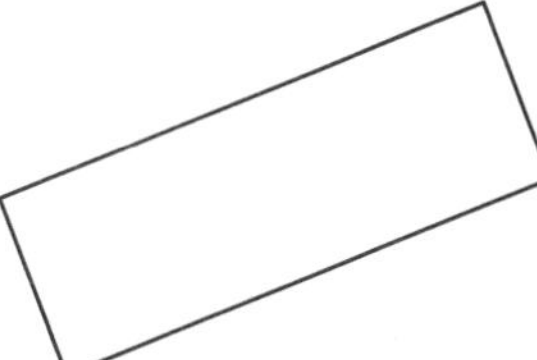
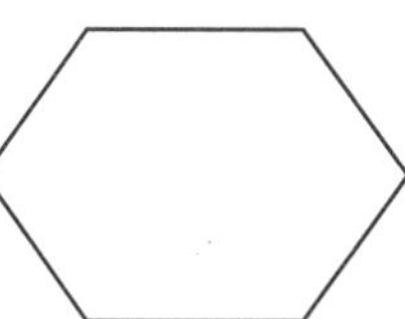
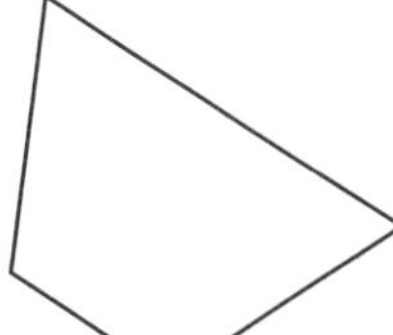

Name: ______________________ Date: ______________

Answer the question.

5. How many letters in each of these words have rotational symmetry and line symmetry?

UNITED STATES OF AMERICA

_______ _______ _______ _______

Draw.

6. Gillian folds a piece of paper and cuts out a shape as shown. Draw the shape when the paper is unfolded.

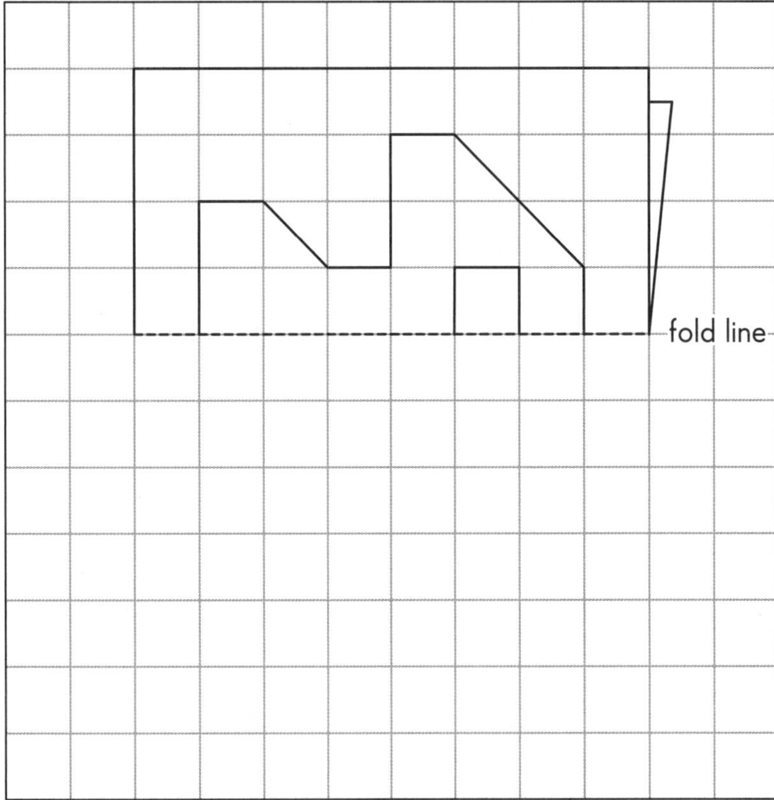

Name: ______________________ Date: ______________

Shade and draw.

7. Shade 9 squares so that the figure has a line of symmetry.
Draw the line of symmetry.

Name: ______________________ Date: ______________

Solve.

8. After rotating a $\frac{1}{4}$-turn counterclockwise, a $\frac{3}{4}$-turn clockwise, and another $\frac{1}{2}$-turn clockwise about point *O*, figure A rests in this final position. Draw the original position of figure A.

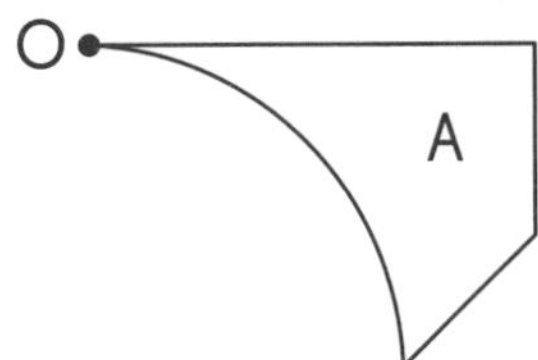

9. Felicia is making a pattern using symmetric shapes.
She has made three designs.
How many squares will she need to make the fifth design?

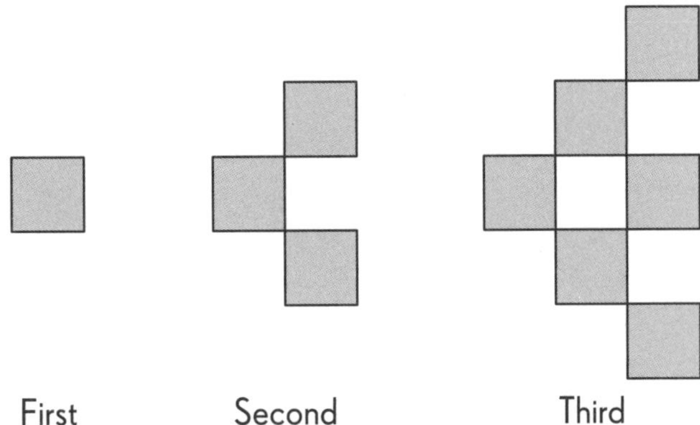

Name: ______________________ **Date:** ______________

Exploration

Draw.

10. Jack and Jade play a game. Jack starts by drawing a square on a grid. Jade continues by drawing the least number of squares needed to make the next symmetric figure. They take turns drawing the next symmetric figure. Draw the possible symmetric figures they could draw at each stage.

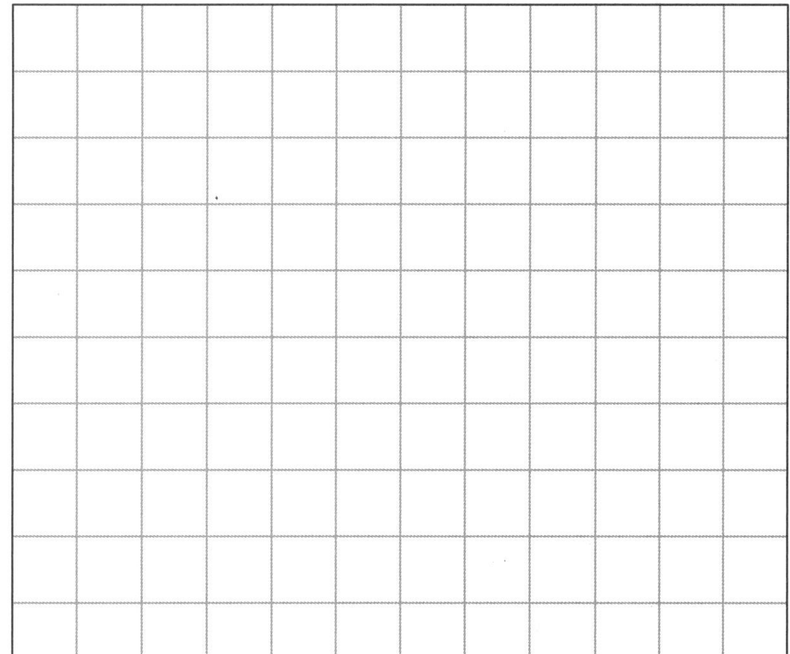

11. In the next game, Jade begins with a triangle. Draw the possible symmetric figures they could draw at each stage.

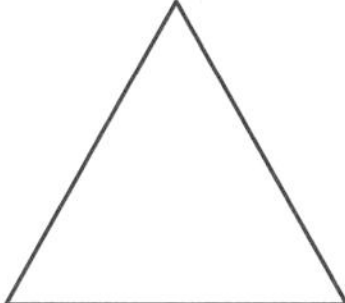

Name: ______________________ Date: ______________

Draw.

12. Draw 3 figures that have rotational symmetry.

Name: ______________________ Date: ______________

Write the steps.

13. The figure shows only half of a symmetric shape.
Write the steps needed to complete the symmetric figure.

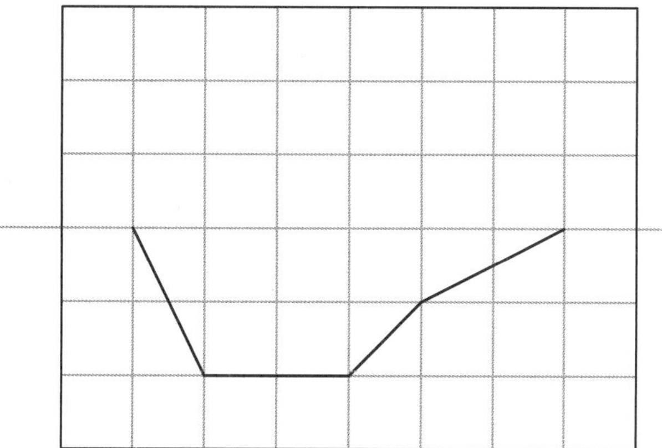

Step 1 ______________________

____

Step 2 ______________________

____

Step 3 ______________________

____

Step 4 ______________________

____

Name: ______________________ Date: ______________

Write the steps.

14. The figure shows a symmetric shape. Write the steps used to find a line of symmetry.

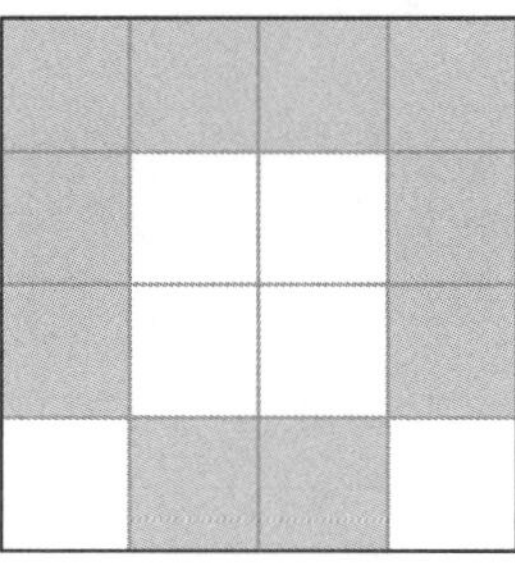

Step 1 ______________________________

____

Step 2 ______________________________

____

Step 3 ______________________________

____

Step 4 ______________________________

____

Name: ________________________ Date: ____________

Tessellations

Thinking Skills

Solve.

1. Mr. Carter wants to put tiles of only one shape in his bathroom. The tiles must fit together so that there are no gaps in between them. Which of the following shapes can Mr. Carter use?

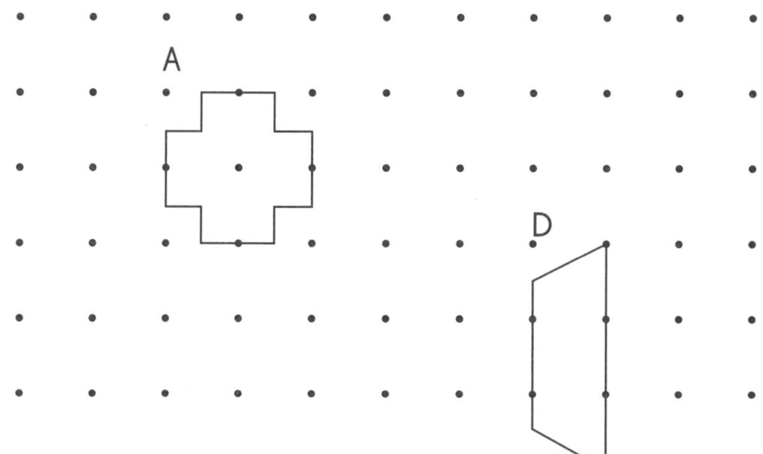

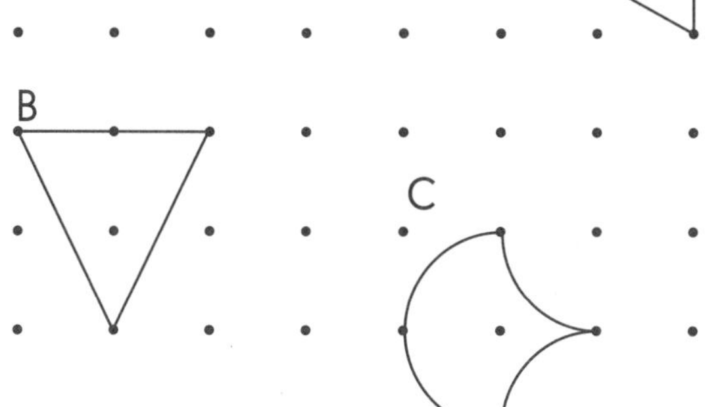

Name: ______________________ Date: ______________

2. Use the shape to make a tessellation in the space provided.

Name: ______________________ Date: ______________

3. Use the shape to make a tessellation in the space provided.

Name: ______________________ Date: ______________

4. Use the shape to make four different tessellations in the space provided.

a. Tessellation 1

Name: ______________________ **Date:** ______________

b. Tessellation 2

Name: ______________________ **Date:** ______________

c. Tessellation 3

Name: ______________________ Date: ______________

d. Tessellation 4

Name: ______________________ Date: ______________

5. The tessellation was formed using Unit Shape A. Identify and outline all the unit shapes within the tessellation.

Unit Shape A

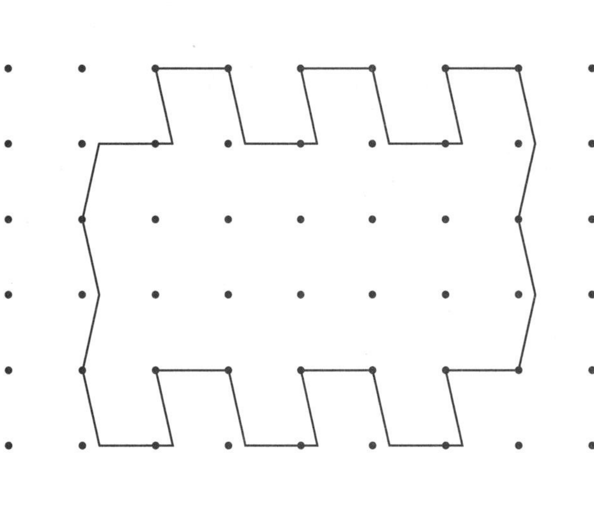

Name: ______________________ **Date:** ______________

Solve.

6. Charlie has a rectangular plot of land. He wants to divide his land equally among his eight children. The first figure below shows the shape of the plot of land each child will receive. On the grid, show how Charlie should distribute the land among his children.

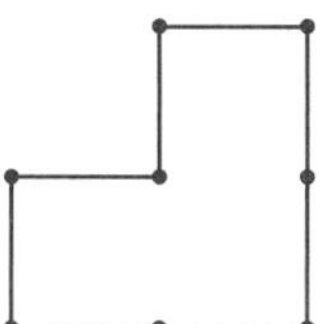

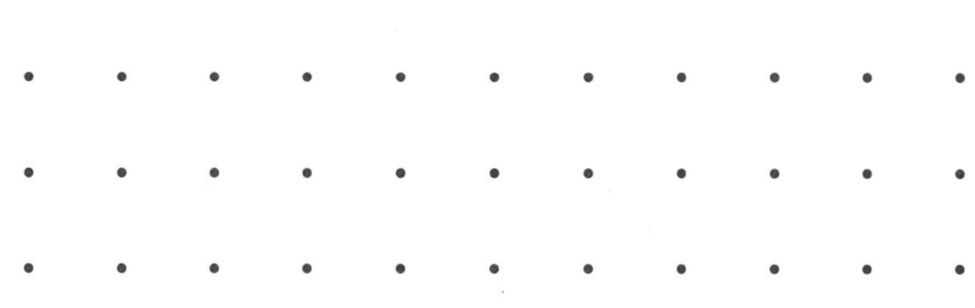

Name: ______________________ **Date:** ______________

Answer the questions.

7. John uses matchsticks to make a tessellation.

a. How many matchsticks will he need to form figure S6?

b. Which figure is formed with 125 matchsticks?

S1

S2

S3

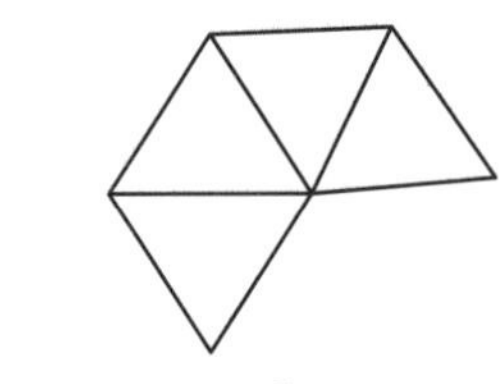
S4

Name: ______________________ **Date:** ______________

Solve. Show your work.

8. A tessellation was made from toothpicks. After some unit shapes were removed from the tessellation, the tessellation was left with the unit shapes shown. How many toothpicks were used to form the original tessellation?

Name: ______________________ Date: ______________

Exploration

Tessellate the shape in two different ways.

9.

Tessellation 1

Tessellation 2

Name: ______________________ **Date:** ______________

Tessellate the shape in two different ways.

10. 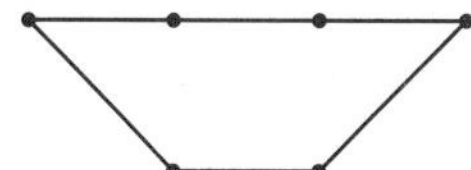

Tessellation 1

Tessellation 2

Name: ______________________ Date: ______________

Tessellate the shape in two different ways.

11. 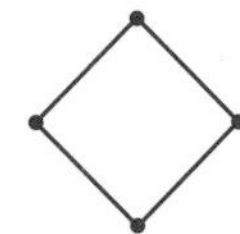

Tessellation 1

Tessellation 2

Name: ______________________ Date: ______________

Explain.

12. Explain why the shape does not tessellate when used in figure A but does tessellate when used in figure B.

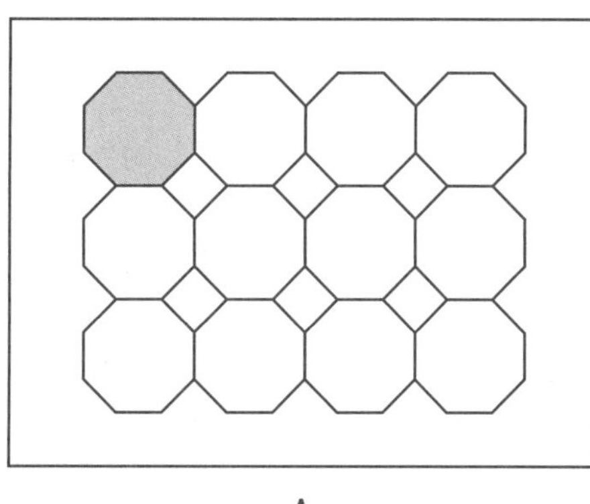

A

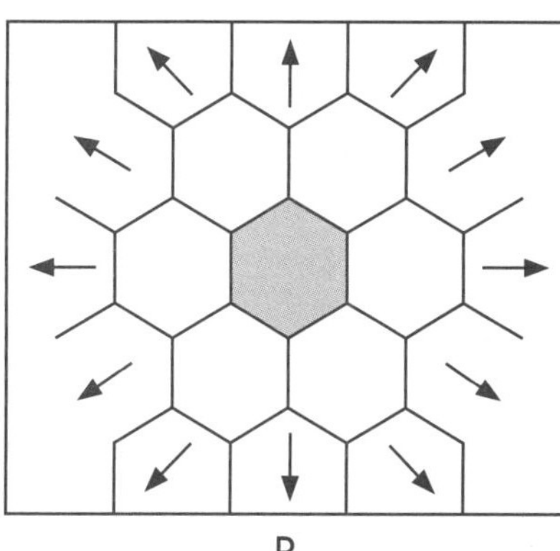

B

____

____

____

13. The first shape is a parallelogram that can tessellate.
Explain how you can form the second shape, which can also tessellate, from the first shape.

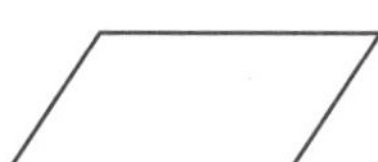

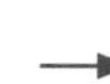

____

____

____

Answers

Chapter 7

1. Solution: 10.7
2. Thinking skill: Deduction
   Solution: 2.85
3. Solution: 2.9
4. Thinking skills: Comparing, Sequencing
   Solution: 6.1, $6\frac{1}{4}$, $6\frac{1}{2}$, 6.9
5. Thinking skills: Comparing, Sequencing
   Solution: $7\frac{2}{5}$, 7.2, $6\frac{3}{5}$, 6.5
6. Thinking skill: Identifying patterns and relationships
   Solution: Accept answers ranging from 1.05 meters to 1.14 meters.
7. Thinking skill: Comparing
   Solution:
   a. 0.05 more than 4.68 is 4.73.
   b. 0.6 less than 2.98 is 2.38.
   c. 0.06 less than 8.33 is 8.27.
   d. 0.7 more than 7.5 is 8.2.
   e. 0.09 more than 1.93 is 2.02.
   f. 0.08 less than 9.12 is 9.04.
   g.

D	E	C	I	M	A	L
2.02	4.68	0.9	0.7	2.38	9.12	8.33

8. Strategy: Look for patterns
   Solution: 7.65, $8\frac{7}{10}$
9. Strategy: Work backward
   Solution:
   20 cents more than $0.80 is $1.
   25 cents more than $1 is $1.25.
   75 cents more than $1.25 is $2.
   Louis had $2 at first.
10. Strategy: Use a diagram
    Solution:
    0.2 more than 0.86 = 1.06
    0.05 more than 1.06 = 1.11
    Leon is 1.11 meters tall.
11. 3 ones and 2 tenths 7 hundredths
    32 tenths and 7 hundredths
    327 hundredths
12. 4 ones and 5 tenths 7 hundredths
    17 thousandths
    4 ones and 4 tenths 18 hundredths
    7 thousandths
    3 ones and 15 tenths 8 hundredths
    7 thousandths
13. 0.58, 0.69, 0.80, 0.91, 1.02;
    0.36, 0.47, 0.58, 0.69, 0.80;
    0.47, 0.58, 0.69, 0.80, 0.91
14. In 14.238, the value of the digit 1 is 1 ten, and the value of the digit 3 is 3 hundredths.
15. 2.409 is the same as 2 ones and 4 tenths 9 thousandths.
16. Answers vary. Samples: 9.3 more than 0.2 is different from 9.3 > 0.2.
    9.3 more than 0.2 is the same as 9.3 + 0.2.
17. 0.75; 0.86
    Add 0.11 to each decimal.
18. 7.23; 6.99
    Subtract 0.24 from each decimal.
19. 0.48; 0.96
    Multiply each decimal by 2.

Chapter 8

1. Thinking skills: Analyzing parts and whole, Identifying patterns and relationships
   Solution: A = 1; B = 2; C = 3; D = 5
   1.32 + 2.23 = 3.55
2. Thinking skills: Comparing, Analyzing parts and whole, Identifying patterns and relationships
   Solution:

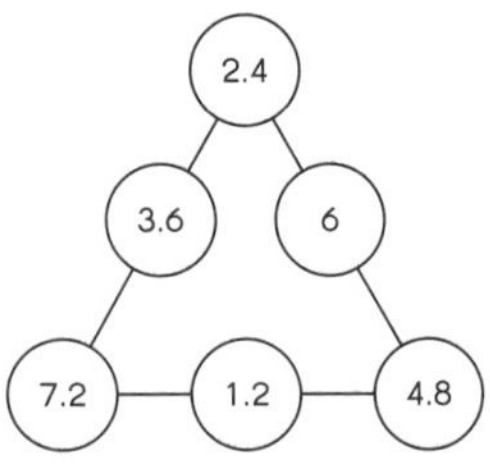

3. Thinking skills: Classifying, Analyzing parts and whole
   Solution:
   $2.50 + $2.50 + $2.50 + $2.50 + $4.00 = $14.00
   Mr. Spencer had to pay $14.00 to park his car.

4. Thinking skill: Analyzing parts and whole

Solution:
\$50 − \$4.30 − \$1.25 − \$3.45 = \$41
She had \$41 left.

5. Thinking skill: Comparing

Solution:
\$3.50 − \$2.32 = \$1.18
A can of tuna is \$1.18 cheaper than a can of fruit cocktail.

6. Thinking skill: Analyzing parts and whole

Solution:
\$3.50 + \$3.50 + \$0.95 + \$2.32 + \$11.27 + \$11.27 = \$32.81
Mrs. Kemery spent \$32.81 altogether.

7. Strategy: Use a model

Solution:

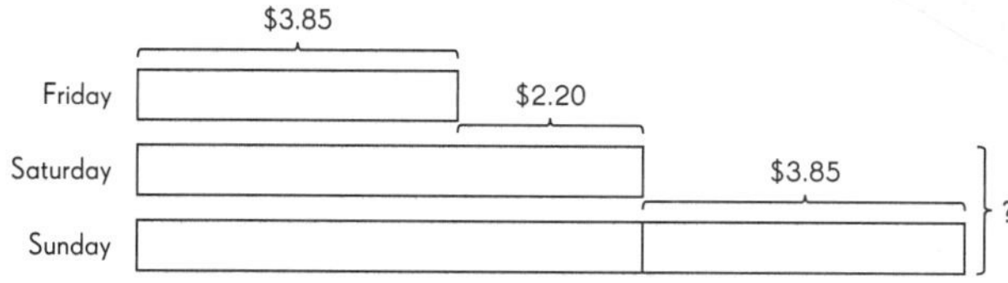

Friday: \$3.85
Saturday: \$3.85 + \$2.20 = \$6.05
Sunday: \$3.85 + \$6.05 = \$9.90
\$6.05 + \$9.90 = \$15.95
Morgan saved \$15.95 altogether on Saturday and Sunday.

8. Strategy: Work backward

Solution:
2.75 + 1.42 + 1.35 − 0.95 = 4.57
Mrs. Blaine bought 4.57 pounds of chicken.

9. Strategy: Use a diagram

Solution:

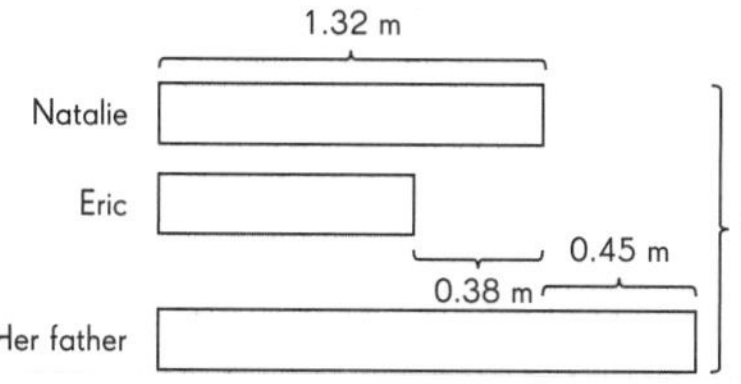

Eric: 1.32 − 0.38 = 0.94
Father: 1.32 + 0.45 = 1.77
1.32 + 0.94 + 1.77 = 4.03
The total height of the three of them is 4.03 meters.

10. A = 0; B = 1; C = 8
A = 1; B = 0; C = 8
A = 2; B = 9; C = 7
A = 3; B = 8; C = 7
A = 5; B = 6; C = 7
A = 6; B = 5; C = 7
A = 8; B = 3; C = 7
A = 9; B = 2; C = 7
If the sum of A and B is 1, then C must be 8.
If the sum of A and B is 11, then C must be 7.

11. X = 1; Y = 0; Z = 4
X = 2; Y = 0; Z = 5
X = 3; Y = 0; Z = 6
X = 4; Y = 0; Z = 7
X = 5; Y = 0; Z = 8
X = 6; Y = 0; Z = 9
To get 1 in the hundredths place, the value of Y must be 0.
X and Z always have a difference of 3, with $X < Z$.

12. 1 – Add the hundredths.
No regrouping is required.
2 – Add the tenths.
3 – Regroup the tenths.
4 – Add the ones.

13. **Step 1:** Write the numbers in vertical form. Line up the decimal points.

Step 2: Add the hundredths.
Regroup the hundredths.
3 + 7 + 5 + 5 + 6 + 4
= 30 hundredths
= 3 tenths

Step 3: Add the tenths.
Regroup the tenths.
8 + 1 + 4 + 5 + 9 + 0 + 3
= 30 tenths = 3 ones

Step 4: Add the ones.
0 + 0 + 0 + 0 + 0 + 0 + 3
= 3 ones

14. **Step 1:** Regroup 4 tenths 7 hundredths.
4 tenths 7 hundredths
= 3 tenths 17 hundredths

Step 2: Subtract the hundredths.
17 − 8 = 9

Step 3: Regroup 1 one and 3 tenths.
1 one and 3 tenths
= 13 tenths

Step 4: Subtract the tenths.
13 tenths − 9 tenths = 4 tenths

Chapter 9

1. Thinking skills: Comparing, Spatial visualization
   Solution:
   Figure A: 4; Figure B: 1
   $4 - 1 = 3$
   There are 3 more angles.
2. Thinking skills: Comparing, Sequencing
   Solution:
   $\angle b$ (45°), $\angle c$ (70°), $\angle e$ (90°), $\angle d$ (130°), $\angle a$ (150°)
3. Thinking skill: Spatial visualization
   Solution:
   $1\frac{1}{4}$-turn: 15 minutes
   5.20 P.M. to 6.05 P.M.: $3\frac{1}{4}$-turns
   6.05 P.M. to 7.05 P.M.: $4\frac{1}{4}$-turns
   So, the total is $7\frac{1}{4}$-turns.
   The minute hand moved through $7\frac{1}{4}$-turns during this time.
4. Thinking skill: Comparing
   Solution:
   $90° + 60° = 150°$
   The measure of the new angle drawn is 150°.
5. Thinking skill: Analyzing parts and whole
   Solution:

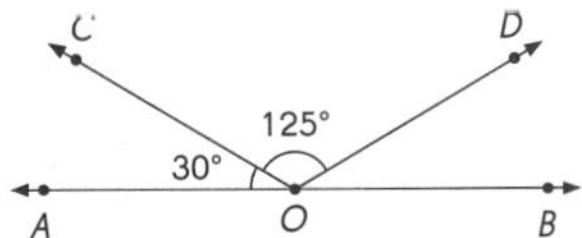

   $180° - 30° - 125° = 25°$
   The measure of $\angle DOB$ is 25°.
6. Strategy: Use a model
   Solution:

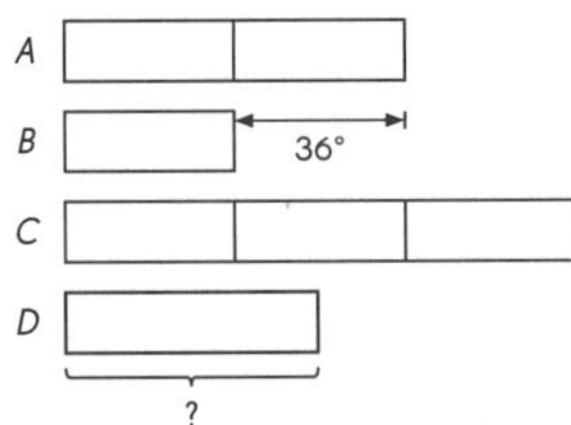

   $36° \times 3 = 108°$
   $108° \div 2 = 54°$
   The measure of angle D is 54°.
7. Strategy: Work backward
   Solution:

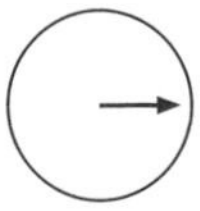

8. Answers vary. Samples:
   $\frac{1}{4}$-turn counterclockwise;
   $\frac{1}{2}$-turn counterclockwise followed by $\frac{1}{4}$-turn clockwise;
   $\frac{1}{2}$-turn clockwise followed by $\frac{3}{4}$-turn counterclockwise
9. 235°
   Methods for finding the angle measure vary.
   Sample:
   Extend one ray to cut the angle into two smaller angles. Measure each angle. The sum of the two angle measures is the unknown angle measure.
10. 2; 4; 3; 1

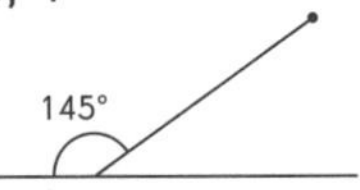

11. Answers vary.
    Sample:
    Move from point A to point F, make a $\frac{1}{4}$-turn clockwise, move from point F to point L, make a $\frac{1}{4}$-turn counterclockwise, move from point L to point K.

Chapter 10

1. Thinking skill: Use a diagram
   Solution: H L E F
2. Thinking skill: Use a diagram
   Solution: I M W H
3. Thinking skill: Comparing
   Solution: $\overline{EH}$
4. Thinking skill: Comparing
   Solution: a; c
5. Thinking skill: Comparing
   Solution: 2
6. Thinking skill: Spatial visualization
   Solution:

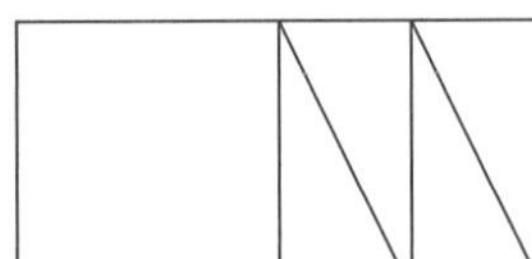

7. Thinking skill: Spatial visualization
   Solution:

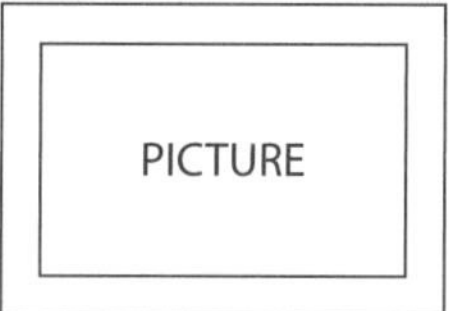

8. Thinking skill: Spatial visualization
   Solution:

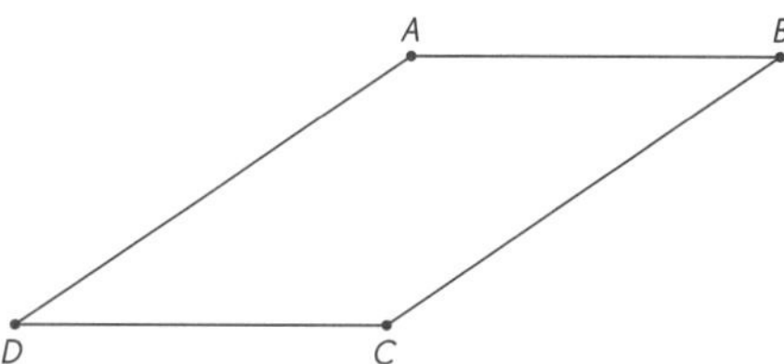

9. Thinking skill: Spatial visualization
   Solution:
   Check that the students draw the correct figure.

10. Strategy: Look for patterns
    Solution: 16
    D1 – 4
    D2 – 6
    D3 – 8
    D4 – 10
    D5 – 12
    D6 – 14
    D7 – 16

11. Strategy: Guess and check
    Solution: 6

Figure	No.	HL	VL	9 Figures?	21 HL?	36 VL?
A B	3 6	6 18	15 12	yes	no	no
A B	5 4	10 12	25 8	yes	no	no
A B	6 3	12 9	30 6	yes	yes	yes

12. 2 squares

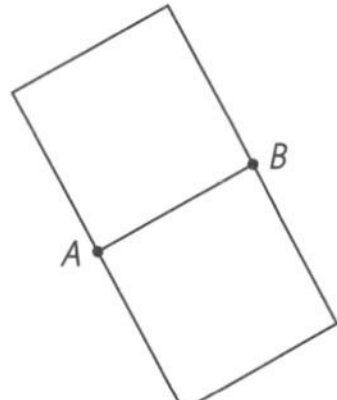

13. Answers vary. Sample:

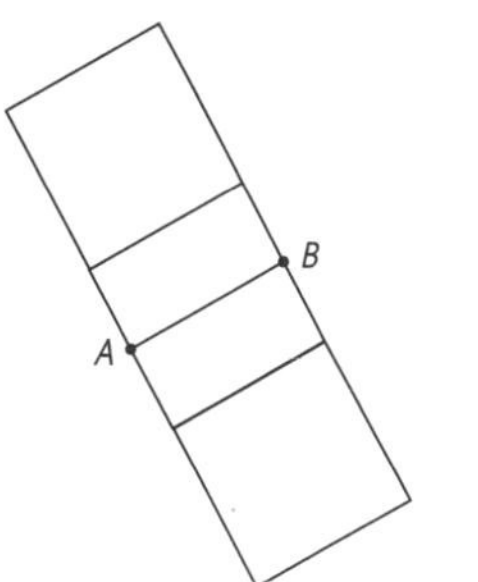

14.

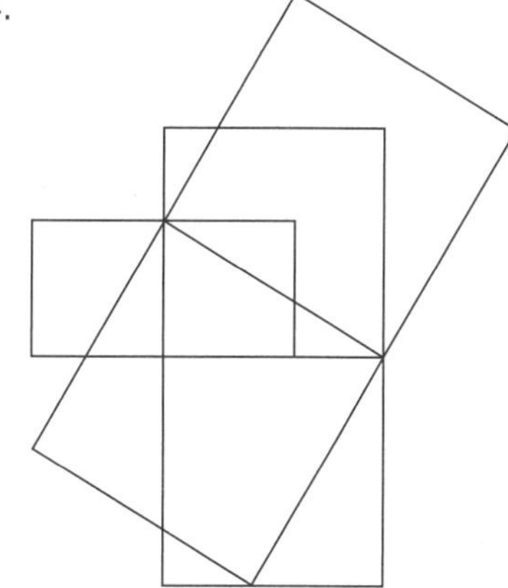

15. Parallel line segments:

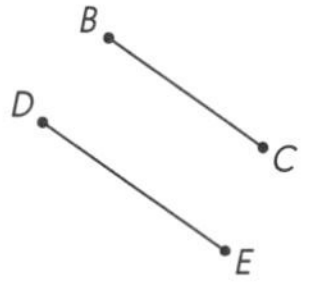

Place a drawing triangle against $\overline{BC}$.
Then place a straightedge at the base of the drawing triangle.
Slide the drawing triangle along the straightedge.
Use the edge of the drawing triangle to draw $\overline{DE}$.
$\overline{BC}$ and $\overline{DE}$ are parallel.

Perpendicular line segments:

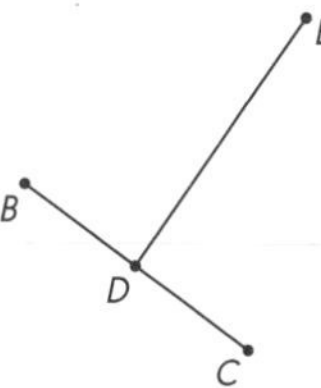

Mark a point on $\overline{BC}$ and label it *D*.
Place the center of the baseline of the protractor on point *D*.
Mark a point at the 90° mark and label it *E*.
Use the edge of the protractor to connect point *E* and point *D*.
$\overline{BC}$ and $\overline{DE}$ are perpendicular.

16. The shape has three pairs of parallel sides: $\overline{AB}$ and $\overline{ED}$, $\overline{BC}$ and $\overline{FE}$, $\overline{AF}$ and $\overline{CD}$.
It has no perpendicular sides.

17. Answers vary.

Chapter 11

1. Thinking skills: Analyzing parts and whole, Identifying patterns and relationships

   Solution:
   Width = 96 ÷ 6 = 16 cm
   Perimeter of 1 rectangle = 6 × 16 = 96 cm
   Perimeter of 2 rectangles = 2 × 96 = 192 cm

2. Thinking skill: Analyzing parts and whole

   Solution:
   Length of $\overline{EC}$ = Length of $\overline{CH}$ = 3 cm
   Length of $\overline{BE}$ = 18 − 3 = 15 cm
   Total = 15 + 6 + 3 = 24 cm
   The total length is 24 cm.

3. Thinking skill: Analyzing parts and whole

   Solution:
   Length of tool shed = 54 ÷ 3 = 18 m
   Width of tool shed = 28 ÷ 4 = 7 m
   Total length of fencing
   = 54 + 54 + 28 + 28 + 7 + 7 − 4
   = 174 m
   The school must order 174 meters of fencing.

4. Thinking skill: Analyzing parts and whole

   Solution:
   Perimeter of square *EFGH*
   = 4 × 9 = 36 cm
   Perimeter of rectangle *ABCD*
   = 2 × 36 = 72 cm
   Length of $\overline{AB}$ = (72 − 6 − 6) ÷ 2 = 30 cm

5. Thinking skill: Analyzing parts and whole

   Solution:
   Total = 2 × 15 + 4 × 1 + 2 × 12 + 4 × 2
   = 30 + 4 + 24 + 8
   = 66 cm
   The total length is 60 centimeters.

6. Thinking skill: Spatial visualization

   Solution:
   90° − 25° = 65°
   2 × 65° = 130°
   The sum of the measures is 130°.

7. Strategy: Use a diagram

   Solution:
   90° − 27° = 63°
   63° ÷ 3 = 21°
   $\angle a$ = 2 × 21° = 42°

8. Strategy: Use a model

   Solution:

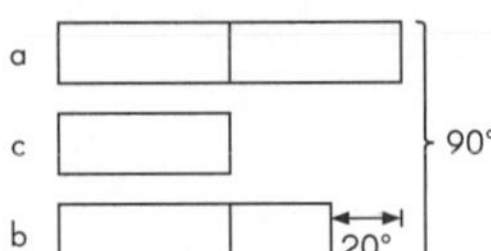

   90° + 20° = 110°
   110° ÷ 5 = 22°
   a → 2 × 22° = 44°
   b → 44° − 20° = 24°
   44° + 24° = 68°
   The sum of the measures is 68°.

9. 16 rectangles; 7 squares

10. Answers vary. Sample:

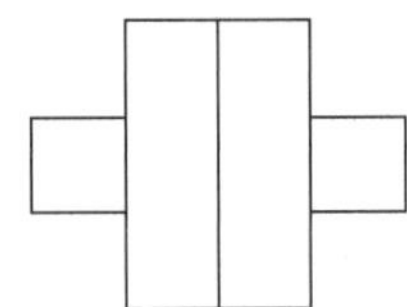

11. Answers vary. Sample figures:

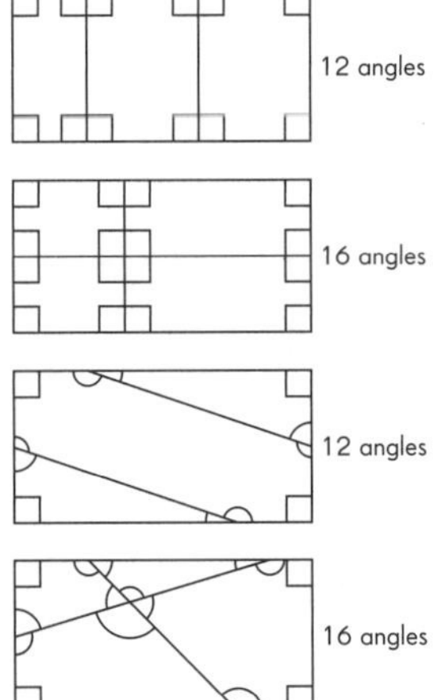

12. Properties of a square:
    - All sides have equal length.
    - Opposite sides are parallel.
    - All angles measure 90°.

    Properties of a rectangle:
    - Opposite sides have equal length.
    - Opposite sides are parallel.
    - All angles measure 90°.

13. $GH + AB = FE + DC$
GH + 5 cm = 7 cm + 1 cm
GH + 5 cm = 8 cm
GH = 3 cm
$AH + GF = BC + DE$
5 cm + 3 cm = 1 cm + DE
8 cm = 1 cm + DE
DE = 7 cm

Chapter 12

1. Thinking skill: Spatial visualization
Solution:
$12 \times 9 = 108$
The total length of all the edges of the cube is 108 centimeters.

2. Thinking skill: Identifying patterns and relationships
Solution:
10 units → 140 cm
1 unit → 14 cm
Length = 4 × 14 = 56 cm
Width = 14 cm
Area = 56 × 14 = 784 cm^2

3. Thinking skill: Analyzing parts and whole
Solution:
Once around the field = 65 + 65 + 15 + 15
= 160 meters
$800 \div 160 = 5$
Jack must run around the field 5 times.

4. Thinking skill: Analyzing parts and whole
Solution:
Perimeter = 28 + 14 + 6 + 6 + 6 + 14 + 6 + 14 + 14 = 108 cm

5. Thinking skills: Analyzing parts and whole, Identifying patterns and relationships
Solution:
13 ÷ 4 is about 3.
9 ÷ 4 is about 2.
$3 \times 2 = 6$
About 6 squares can be cut from the piece of paper.

6. Thinking skills: Analyzing parts and whole, Identifying patterns and relationships
Solution:
$768 \div 6 = 128$
$16 \times 8 = 128$
Perimeter = 16 + 8 + 16 + 8 = 48 cm

7. Strategy: Work backward
Solution:
$6 - 4 = 2$
$36 \div 2 = 18$
$18 - 6 = 12$
Perimeter = 12 + 2 + 12 + 2 = 28 cm

8. Strategy: Guess and check
Solution:
Length of rectangle A = 12 cm
Length of rectangle B = 8 cm

A			B			Area of A between 60 and 100 cm^2?
L	W	A	L	W	A	
6	4	24	4	3	12	no
9	6	54	6	$4\frac{1}{2}$	27	no
12	8	96	8	6	48	yes

9. Strategy: Look for patterns
Solution:
$9 = 3 \times 3$
$3 \times 2 = 6$
$6 \times 2 = 12$
$12 \times 2 = 24$
$4 \times 24 = 96$
The perimeter of the largest square is 96 centimeters.

10. 14 cm; no

Figure	1	2	3	4	5	6
Area	12	12	12	12	12	12
Length	12	6	4	—	—	—
Width	1	2	3	—	—	—
Perimeter	26	16	14	—	—	—

11. 26 cm; no

12. With the same area, the greater the length of a figure, the greater its perimeter.

13. Answers vary. Sample:

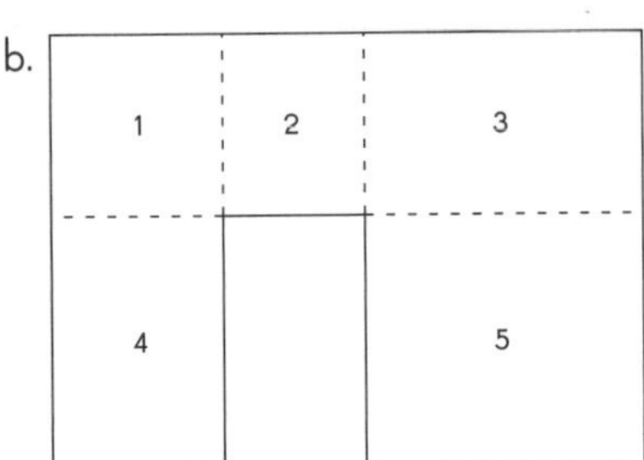

14. $AF = BC + DE = 7$ cm
$EF = AB + CD = 21$ cm
Perimeter $= 7 + 21 + 7 + 21 = 56$ cm

15. $48 - 3 - 3 = 42$
$24 - 3 - 3 = 18$
$42 \times 18 = 756$
The area of the inner rectangle is 756 square centimeters.

Chapter 13

1. Thinking skill: Spatial visualization
Solution:

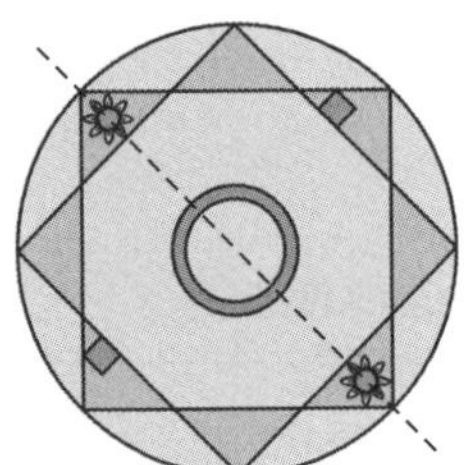

2. Thinking skill: Spatial visualization
Solution: 8

3. Thinking skill: Spatial visualization
Solution:

Answers vary. Sample:

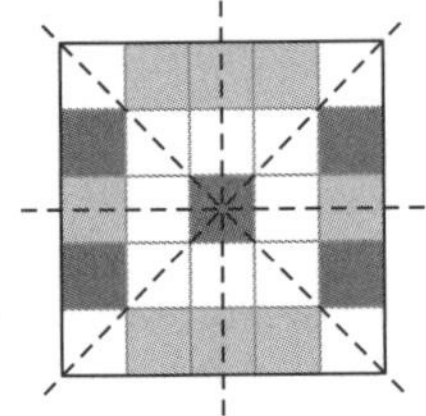

4. Thinking skill: Spatial visualization
Solution:

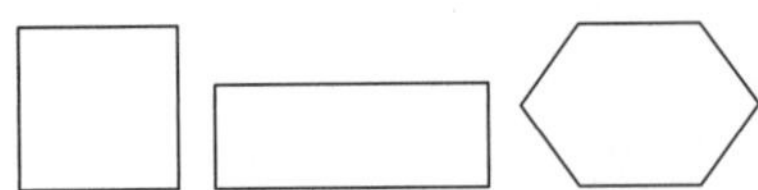

5. Thinking skills: Classifying, Spatial visualization
Solution: 1 (I); 0; 1 (O); 1 (I)

6. Thinking skills: Identifying patterns and relationships, Spatial visualization
Solution:

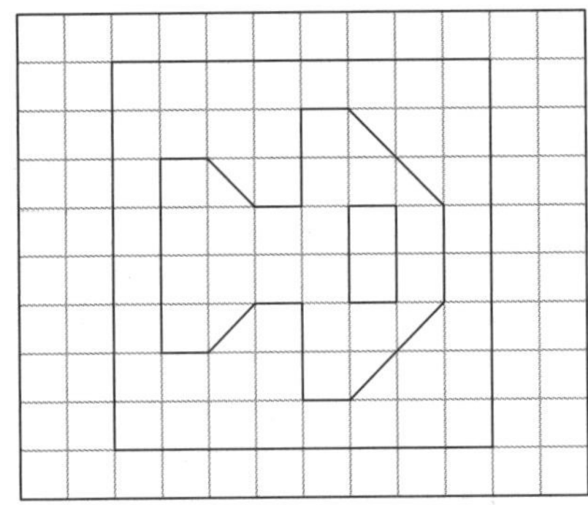

7. Thinking skill: Spatial visualization
Solution:

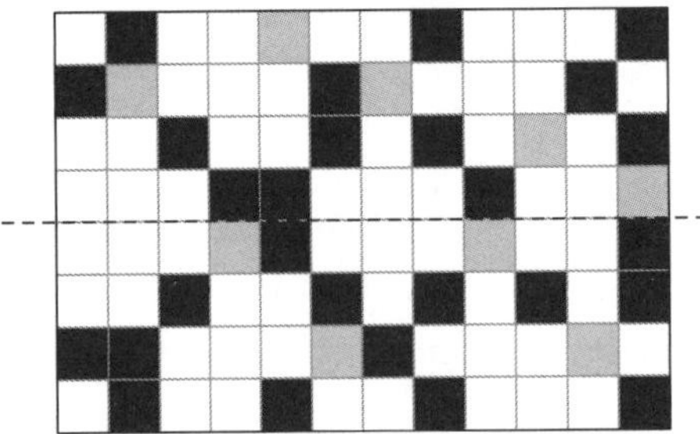

8. Strategy: Work backward
Solution:

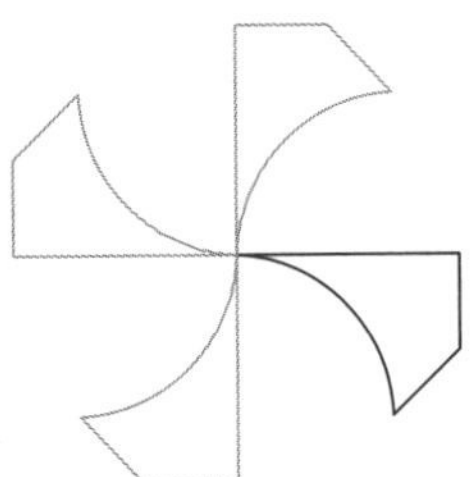

9. Strategy: Look for patterns
Solution: 15 squares
First — 1
Second — 3
Third — 6
Fourth — 10
Fifth — 15

10. Answers vary. Samples:

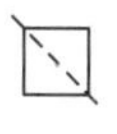 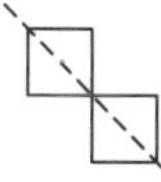 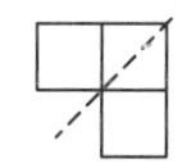

11. Answers vary. Samples:

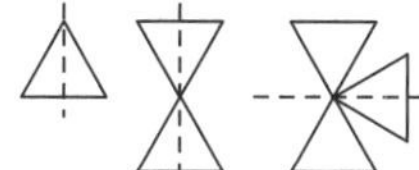

12. Answers vary. Samples:

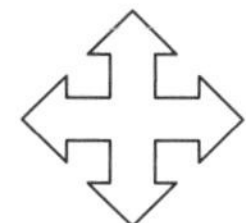 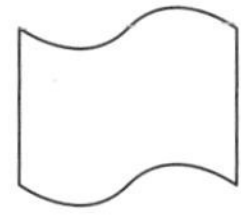 

13.

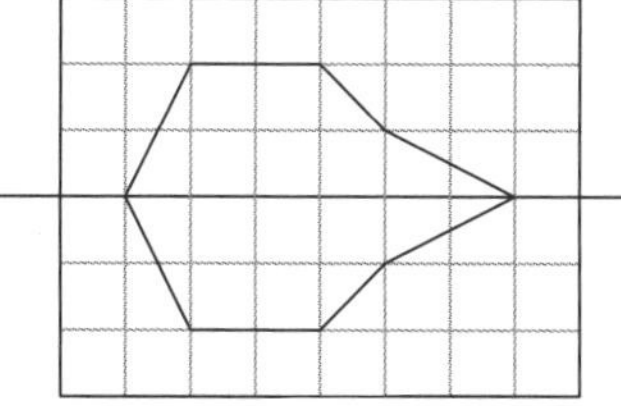

Step 1: Identify the line of symmetry.

Step 2: Look at the existing part of the figure and study it in relation to the line of symmetry.

Step 3: Draw lines above the line of symmetry that are congruent to the lower half of the drawing.

Step 4: Continue drawing until you have completed the symmetric figure.

14. **Step 1:** Copy the figure on a sheet of paper and cut it out.

Step 2: Draw a line across the figure.

Step 3: Fold the figure along this line.

Step 4: Check if the two parts are congruent and match exactly. If they do, then the line you have drawn is a line of symmetry.

Chapter 14

1. Thinking skills: Identifying patterns and relationships, Spatial visualization

Solution: A, B, C, and D are all possible.

2. Thinking skills: Identifying patterns and relationships, Spatial visualization

Solution:

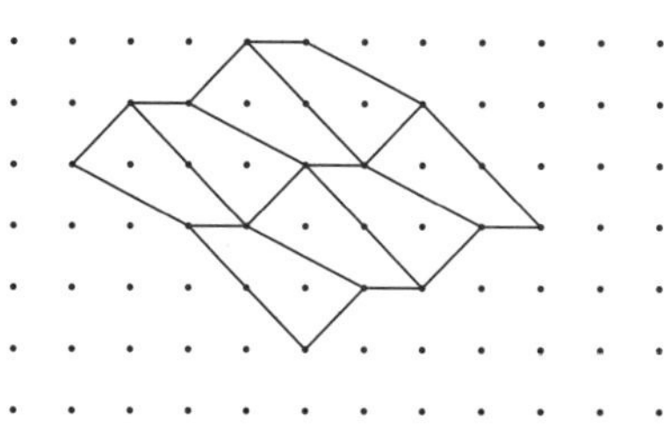

3. Thinking skills: Identifying patterns and relationships, Spatial visualization

Solution:

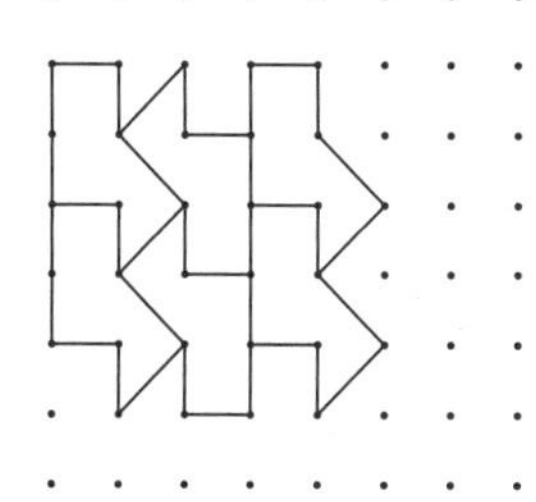

4. Thinking skills: Identifying patterns and relationships, Spatial visualization

Solution: Answers vary. Samples:

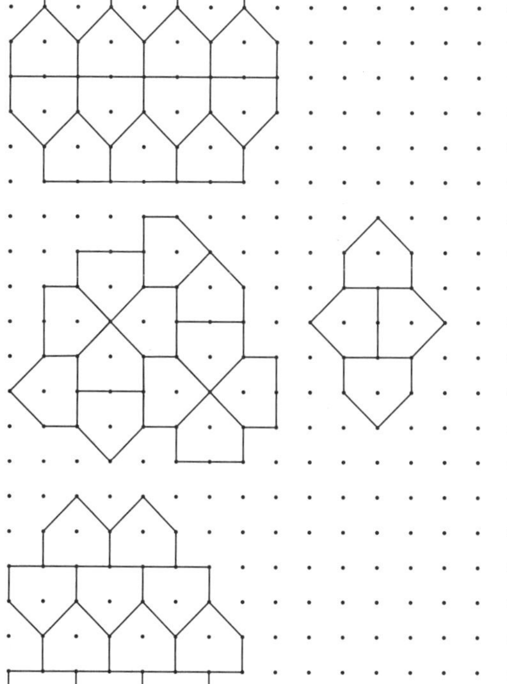

5. Thinking skills: Identifying patterns and relationships, Spatial visualization

Solution:

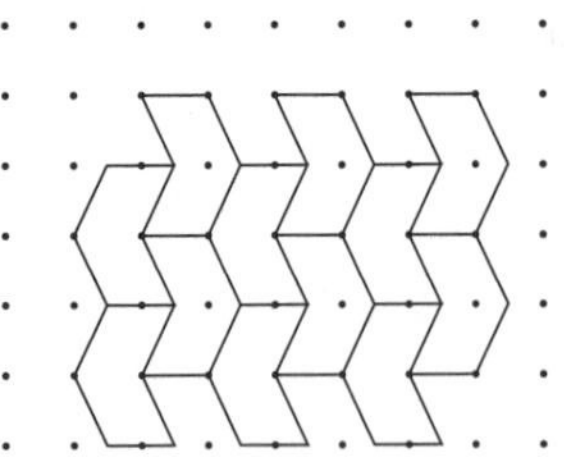

6. Thinking skills: Identifying patterns and relationships, Spatial visualization

Solution: Answers vary. Sample:

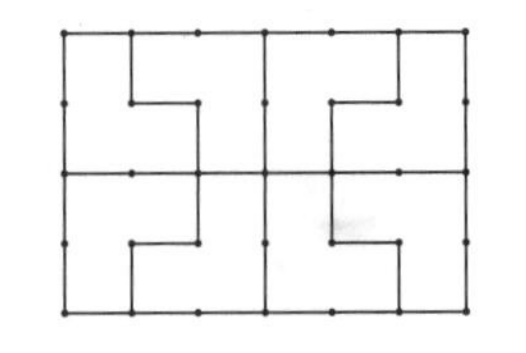

7. Strategy: Look for patterns

Solution:

a. 13 (This is a + 2 pattern.)

$3 + 2 + 2 + 2 + 2 + 2 = 13$

He will need 13 matchsticks to form figure S6.

b. $125 - 1 = 124$

$124 \div 2 = 62$

Figure S62 is formed with 125 matchsticks.

8. Strategy: Simplify the problem

Solution:

6 toothpicks form a hexagon.

There are 7 hexagons in half of the pattern.

$6 \times 7 = 42$

12 of the toothpicks are shared between the hexagons.

$42 - 12 = 30$

There are 2 groups of 7 hexagons in the pattern.

$2 \times 30 = 60$

3 of the toothpicks are shared between the 2 groups of 7 hexagons.

$60 - 3 = 57$

57 toothpicks were used to form the original tessellation.

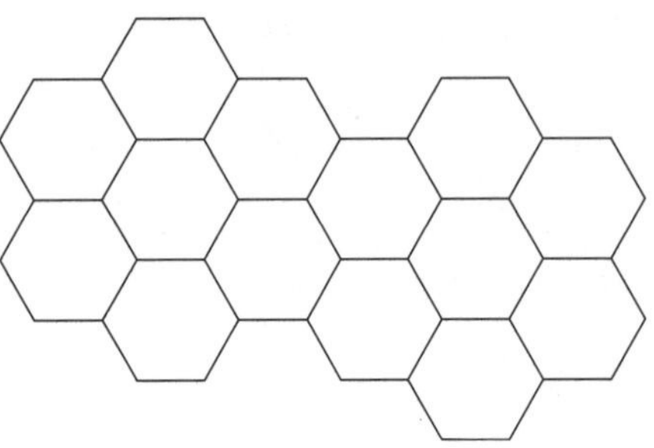

9. Answers vary. Samples:

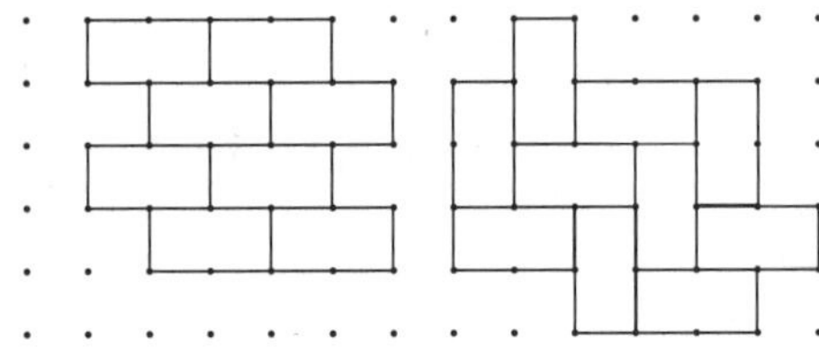

10. Answers vary. Sample:

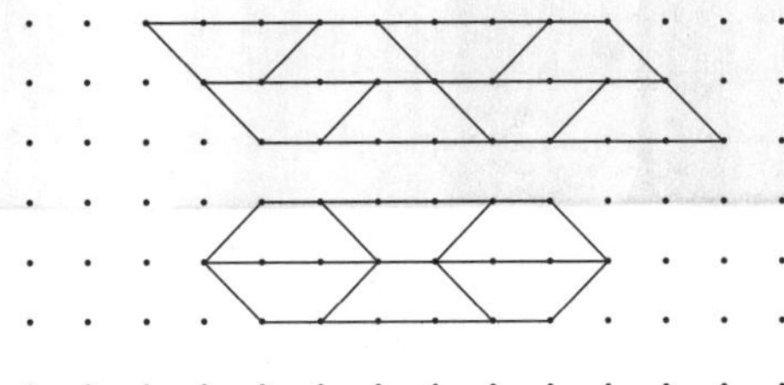

11. Answers vary. Sample:

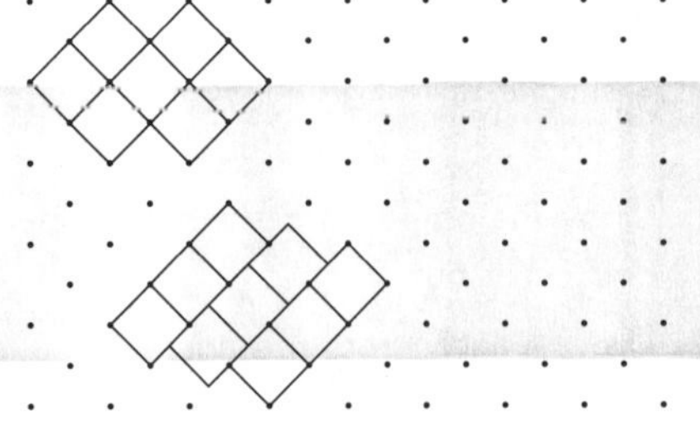

12. In figure A, the shape does not tessellate because there are gaps between the figures. In figure B, the shape tessellates because it covers a surface with no gaps or overlaps between the figures.

13. Cut a triangle on the left end of the parallelogram and move it to the right end.